ADVENTURES IN DARKNESS

ADVENTURES IN DARKNESS

The Summer of an Eleven-Year-Old Blind Boy

TOM SULLIVAN

NELSON BOOKS
A Division of Thomas Nelson Publishers
Since 1798

www.thomasnelson.com

Published in Nashville, Tennessee, by Thomas Nelson, Inc.

Nelson Books titles may be purchased in bulk for educational, business, fundraising, or sales promotional use. For information, please email SpecialMarkets@ThomasNelson.com.

Library of Congress Cataloging-in-Publication Data

Sullivan, Tom, 1947–
    Adventures in darkness : memoirs of an eleven-year-old blind boy / Tom Sullivan.
      p. cm.
    Includes bibliographical references and index.
    ISBN-10: 0-7852-2081-X (hardcover : alk. paper)
    ISBN-13: 978-0-7852-2081-7 (hardcover : alk. paper)
    1. Sullivan, Tom, 1947—Childhood and youth. 2. Children, Blind—United States—Biography. 3. Blind musicians—United States—Biography. I. Title.
HV1792.S854 A3 2006
362.4'1092—dc22
[B]   2006019092

Printed in the United States of America

1 2 3 4 5 6 QW 08 07 06 05

To Billy,
who taught me to play
and helped me win in the game of life

To Perkins School for the Blind,
Despite my greatest childhood efforts
you gave me the education essential
to who I am

TABLE OF CONTENTS

1 ⁞ THE GREAT ESCAPE

JA-JING—STEP, STEP.

Ja-Jing—Step, Step.

Ja-Jing—Step, Step.

Ja-Jing—Step, Step.

I listened to the syncopated rhythms of the fat man as he patrolled the echoing halls of the boarding school, my personal prison. The sound of his leather-soled shoes and heavy key ring framed his every movement, and I knew exactly where he was throughout his nightly rounds. My escape, planned so carefully, was about to begin. Though I was nervous—even a little frightened—the freedom on the other side of the walls was far more important to me than any consequence I might suffer for what I was about to do.

Ja-Jing—Step, Step.

Ja-Jing—Step, Step.

The fat man's feet faded down the corridor. "Okay, guys," I whispered to the darkness. "It's time to go."

"I don't know, Tommy," Jerry's voice whined back. "Maybe this isn't such a good idea. Maybe we oughta just stay right here."

"Shut up, Jerry," Ernie hissed. "Tommy and me have examined every detail of the plan, and it's perfect. If you don't want to go, we're leaving without you. But remember, when they find out we're not here, you'll be the only one left to take the blame."

We heard Jerry sigh, resigned to his fate. "Okay, okay, I'm coming. I don't want to stay here by myself."

I was already at the window, tying off the sheets that we had strung together. I just hoped they were long enough to reach the ground. In every escape, there's stuff you can't be sure of, and I really didn't know exactly how far it was from the window to the earth below. It was early spring in New England, and the moisture of the night had released a potpourri of smells. My spirits soared as I took it all in—lilac, apple blossom, night jasmine, and freshly cut grass—all signaling that the world was out there, just waiting for us to set off on our grand adventure.

Ernie touched my arm. "Okay, Tommy, this is your idea. You go first."

"Oh sure," I laughed. "You just want to know if the sheets will hold."

"I know they'll hold you and me, pal," he said. "What I'm

really interested to find out is what will happen when Fatty Jerry takes the death drop."

"Shut up, you guys," Jerry whined again. "I'm not that fat."

Our snickers told him we didn't agree.

I sat on the ledge of our third-story window with the sheet in both hands and took a deep breath. "Here I go, boys," I said over my shoulder. "Geronimooooooooo!" Swinging out into space, I lowered myself down the bed sheet rope. Ernie had tied all our bed sheets together with sheet bend knots he learned in Boy Scouts, and the material tightened under my weight. Reaching the bottom, I dangled for a moment, wondering just how far it was to the ground. I was relieved to find that I was only a couple of feet from terra firma. "I'm fine," I called up to my compatriots. "It's easy. Come on down."

Less than thirty seconds later, Ernie landed with commando-type grace.

"Okay, Jerry," I stage whispered, "it's your turn."

We waited and felt the sheet continue to wave in the night breeze. Maybe Jerry was chickening out. I added a little more urgency to my voice. "Let's go, Jerry! We haven't got all night!"

"What if I fall?"

"We'll catch you," I said.

"No, we won't," Ernie laughed. "Do you know what his fat butt would do to us in free-fall? We'd be smooshed."

Jerry was still whining. "What about my food? I can't find my food!"

I reached into my backpack and pulled out a paper bag,

shaking it like I was signaling to Pavlov's dog. "I have your food, Fatty! Now, come on, or we're going to leave you, and I know you wouldn't really want that!"

"All right," he quavered, "here I come."

I finally felt the tension on the sheets. His nervous shakings were actually palpable under my fingertips as Jerry suspended himself in space. Unlike Ernie and me, who had descended quickly to the ground, Jerry made his way down painfully, haltingly hand-over-hand, as if he were working his way down the north face of Mount Everest. Then, about six feet from the ground, gravity overcame Jerry's grip and he dropped like a stone, landing in a heap at our feet. Soft spring grass and his ample padding prevented major injury. And after a little more whining, we moved out through the darkness, heading for the fence line at the Charles River.

Like all great escapes, this one had been meticulously planned with conversations whispered deep into the night. We knew exactly how to pull it off. Once outside, we would make our way to the compound's boathouse, where rowboats provided occasional exercise on the river for inmates on good behavior. The lock on the gate would be no problem because of the hacksaw we'd stolen from the prison shop and placed in my backpack, along with a set of wire cutters. All we'd have to do was drag the boat to the river and let the current take us out into Boston Harbor and freedom.

My friend Ernie was a genius. At eleven, he was already taking advanced calculus and physics. By using the almanac to determine times and tides and by dangling a fishing line in the river to calculate the speed of the current, he figured we could voyage to the Atlantic in about seven hours. He went on to elaborate that the current flowed at about two miles an hour, and we could go even faster if we picked a night when the tide was on its way out. So that's exactly what we did.

Nearing the boathouse, we dropped onto our bellies in an extended military crawl. This area of the yard was brightly lit, providing us with the greatest danger of discovery. As I arrived at the corner of the boathouse, feeling Ernie right behind me, Jerry's whines had turned to sniffling.

"What's the matter now, Jerry?" I asked.

"I think I crawled through dog crap."

"You sure did," Ernie confirmed, sniffing loudly and laughing in the dark. "That's dog crap, all right. Probably the excrement of a large German shepherd."

I stifled my own laugh. "You can wash it off in the river when we get there, Jerry. Right now, we've gotta pull this boat out of here."

Finding the boathouse door, I pulled the stolen hacksaw out of my backpack and prepared to go to work on the lock and chain. "Ernie, put your hands on each end of the chain, and keep it from flopping around so I can get a good pull with the blade of the saw."

"Okay, Tommy. I got it. Go ahead."

Placing the saw on the chain where the lock and hasp came together, I began to cut. The screech of the saw was like a siren going off in the night. "Wow," Ernie said. "You're gonna have to do this fast, Tommy, or they'll be right on our butts."

I sawed with all my might and, thank God, the padlock and chain were old. With just a few strokes, they broke and the door swung open. Four dinghies rested on boat stands, and within minutes we dragged one of them out onto the grass in front of the boathouse, tossed our belongings inside, and headed for the river.

The boathouse had been built on a downhill slant right up against the fence that bordered the Charles River. With a lot of grunting and some more complaining from Jerry, we arrived at the fence line. With a little more applied dexterity from Ernie, the wire cutters quickly sliced a hole big enough to fit the bow of the boat through the fence. The next part would take all of our strength. "Okay, guys, this is it," I told my friends. "We can do it. We can get to the river. Ready? Heave!"

All of us grunted, pushing in unison. No progress. Two more tries yielded nothing but a lot of heavy breathing. "I told you this wouldn't work," Jerry complained. "I told you! We should have just stayed in bed. I told you!"

"Listen, Jerry, I promised you and Ernie the best adventure of your life, as good as Huck and Tom, and that's what we're gonna have. We just need to try a little harder. Come on, boys, let's give it everything we've got."

Our Herculean effort was rewarded by the grating sound of the boat crunching through the ever-widening hole in the chain-link fence.

"Keep going," I cried. "We've got it! I know we've got it."

Seconds later, the boat was clear and we clambered through the fence. We could hear the river lapping just a few feet away. I moved forward to the bow. "Okay, guys, let's launch her."

With a couple more pulls and pushes, I stepped into the murky waters of the Charles, feeling the cold of the spring-filled river all the way up to my thighs. "Okay, guys, get in. I'll push us off, and then I'll jump into the stern."

Ernie quickly took his place. Jerry literally fell in like an old sack. "For God's sake, Jerry," Ernie said. "Can't you do anything right?"

"Oh no!" Jerry moaned, pulling himself up. "I fell on top of my food, and it's all crushed." I couldn't stop laughing as I pushed off and jumped in back.

Even though it was pitch dark, it was easy to stay in the middle of the river. The banks were reinforced so the water was constantly gurgling against pylons, docks, and even reinforced concrete. After a few minutes, we were far enough downstream to speak in normal tones, and Ernie called for a cheer.

"Hip, hip, hooray!" we cried in unison.

"We're on our way to foreign lands," I told my fellow travelers.

"Dancing girls," Ernie put in, though we didn't really know what those were.

Even Jerry was optimistic. "Food from foreign places."

Ernie began to sing, "Yo ho, yo ho, a pirate's life for me!" from *Peter Pan*, and we all joined in. That was followed by choruses of "Ninety-Nine Bottles of Beer on the Wall" and some pretty good rock-and-roll in three-part harmony: "Papa-Oom-Mow-Mow," "Duke of Earl," and "Get a Job."

All in all, this escape was going completely according to plan. The next few hours could only be described as blessed freedom, freedom to sing and freedom to dream. The stories got wilder and wilder, and the laughter—oh, the laughter—got sillier and sillier.

A foghorn at the entrance of Boston Harbor was the North Star of our voyage. Night after night it beaconed to us while we planned our escape. Once we reached it, we would have left the confines of the Charles and moved into the vast, open water of the bay. And as dawn was rising in the east, we came abreast of the horn's warning sound.

The poet was right—the plans of mice and men often do go astray, especially the schemes of eleven-year-olds whose only motivation is escape and adventure. The future was something we hadn't even considered. Just as we entered the harbor, Ernie voiced the question we all were thinking, "Now what?" But we didn't have time to think of an answer before we heard a deep-throated rumbling coming toward us out of the fog.

In 1959, Boston was one of the busiest ports in America. Because of its deep channel, freighters and ocean liners could move expediently, especially when, without the aid of tugs, they unlawfully ignored the five-knot limit. The rumble was quickly joined by the sound of propellers slicing a path through the water, seemingly right down on top of us.

The three of us screamed as the freighter bore down, missing us by less than twenty feet. "Hold on," I yelled. "We're gonna be in her wake."

Our twelve-foot dinghy was literally tossed into the air like a twig in a hurricane. By some miracle, we came down on the other side of the wake, still upright, but completely flooded.

"We're sinking," Ernie yelled. "Oh my God, we're sinking!"

"Just bail! Bail!" I yelled back. "Use your hands! Use anything!" As we worked desperately to save the little boat, we became aware of other ships moving through the fog.

Jerry was crying, "We're gonna die out here! We're gonna die!"

At that moment, I couldn't say I disagreed with him. What had begun as a little adventure had evolved into a life-and-death situation, and our earlier fun and boyish bravado had been replaced by panic and fear. The single foghorn was now drowned out by the early morning din of commerce, and we were right in the middle of it—three little boys in a twelve-foot boat, like minnows in a pod of whales.

"Oh God," Ernie said. "Here comes another one." But this time, the speed seemed to slow, and then the pitch of the motor changed.

"They've stopped," Ernie gauged. "For some reason, this one stopped."

The reason became clear as a bullhorn announced, "Ahoy the boat, ahoy the boat! This is the United States Coast Guard. Prepare to accept a tow."

"How do we do that?" I asked Ernie.

"I don't know. I guess they'll tell us."

Something landed on the bow of the little dinghy with a thwack.

"What was that?" Jerry asked, the alarm obvious in his voice.

"I don't know," Ernie said.

Thirty seconds later, the thwack happened again, but still we didn't understand what it meant.

The voice on the bullhorn was speaking again. "You have ignored our tow line. Prepare to be boarded."

"Prepare to be boarded?" I said. "I guess this is the end of our adventure."

The Coast Guard boat had moved in close astern, and in a moment a man landed on the bow of the dinghy.

The surprise was evident in his tone. "What are you boys doing out here in the middle of the shipping lanes? Don't you know you could get killed? And why did you ignore the command to tie off our line and be towed to safety?"

In the early morning light, the way we looked at him must've given us away. We heard his radio crackle. "Captain Edwards, Lieutenant Carson here. Sir, I can't believe it, but what we have out here are three little boys who are"—he paused—"who seem to be"—another beat—"blind."

2 ⦂ DA

Edison, my big German Shepherd, changed positions at my feet as the United Airlines 767 dropped its nose in preparation for the landing. The voice of the flight attendant announced our arrival. "Ladies and Gentlemen, we've begun our descent into Boston's Logan Airport. Please make sure your seats are in the full upright position and that your seatbelts are fastened securely, low and tight across your laps."

We were flying to Boston because of a phone call I'd received the night before from my sister Peggy. Just three words that said so much, "Da is dead."

My father, the giant who had cast his influence over my whole life, was no longer living. Cancer had ravaged his body, and I was sure that death, in its way, had been a blessing. The last time I had seen him, we had gone fishing, and he made it clear that living was becoming much too painful an option.

And so he was gone, and I, the dutiful son, was coming home to oversee his wake and funeral. That had been his wish, made very clear to me a number of times over the last few years. "Make it a grand wake, Tommy," he had told me. "First cabin. Don't cut the Scotch. Give them twelve-year-old, and keep it coming."

So, there I was, taxiing into the terminal, wondering how many skeletons would appear out of the closet and what the many voices from the past would have to say about the life of Thomas Joseph "Porky" Sullivan.

Edison's muzzle brushed against me before he guided me perfectly down the jet way. With a little help from other passengers, we arrived at baggage claim and quickly found my bag on the carousel. The smell tag attached to the handle was easy for the animal to pick out, and in minutes we were outside on the street, greeted by my limo driver, Randy.

Whenever I was in Boston, Randy took care of me. It had been that way for the past twenty years. On this night, my friend could tell I just wanted quiet, as we glided through the Ted Williams Tunnel on the way to the Southeast Expressway that would take us to the secondary roads leading to my boyhood home, Scituate.

Scituate is a seacoast town nestled twenty-eight miles south of Boston. The Irish politicians who inhabit it in the summers refer to it as the Irish Riviera because of its favorable climate, good fishing, and spectacular ocean views. My family had chosen to live there year-round because my father said it reminded him of Kinsale, the village on the west coast of Ireland that had been his boyhood home.

Da would commute to Boston, usually staying in the city for three or four days a week and arriving back home for long weekends. Most of the time, he would pick me up on Fridays when I was released from the blind school. I loved the special hours we shared on the drive, just being a father and a son. We'd talk baseball and Ted Williams, the Celtics and Bill Russell, or he'd tell me stories about growing up in the Irish countryside. "The old country," he'd call it, and I understood early on that it would always be his favorite place.

I had asked him once if he wanted me to bury him back there, under the green Irish sod. "No," he said, "Ireland may have been the old country, but it was America that provided me with opportunity, Tommy, so it's here I'll stay."

"Here" was to be a burial plot in St. Mary's Cemetery, shared with my mother even though their marriage had ended many years ago. How strange their moral compass was, their direction confused by the polarization of faith and guilt, honesty and lies, public face and private passions.

My mother had died five years ago. I had remained close to her all through her life, and had taken care of her in her latter years. We always regarded each other as mother and son, rather than friends. And this was okay because in her generation, that's the way it was. Now, as we drove down the Southeast

Expressway, I pondered my relationship with my father. On the surface, we were great friends, and yet I had to admit that I had always been afraid of him.

Randy had turned the car off the Southeast Expressway onto Route 123, the two-lane country road that would take us to Driftway and Scituate Harbor. Only in New England would two-lane roads be given designations like superhighways. These were the old roads, dating back to Revolutionary times. This windy thoroughfare never lets you go faster than thirty-five miles an hour. But on this night, I loved that, as I put my head out the window and listened to the sounds of early summer crickets and evening robins saying good night to the day.

Turning left onto Driftway, the town of Scituate and all it meant to me came into sensory focus. The breeze off the Atlantic, I breathed it, inhaled it, pulled it deep into my lungs, allowing the salt air to nourish my spirit. This ocean was age-less in its ebb and flow of time and tide. I breathed in the ocean pungency: the kelp clinging to sedimentary stone, single-cell forms of life being created every second, and drying seaweed and sea creatures gone aground.

There were familiar land smells as we passed through the neighborhood as well—fresh cut grass, roses planted by loving hands in gardens bordering the street, late spring lilac and early summer fertilizing added to the complex sauce that I drew in, tasted, and smelled.

Randy was turning onto Front Street, the main street of Scituate Harbor, and I heard it: the sound that had defined my getting up and my going to sleep, the sound that said fair weather or foul to fishermen and boaters, the sound that marked the syncopated rhythm necessary for all of us to know that we are alive. It was the sound of the old bell buoy ringing five miles out off the point of Scituate Harbor. I was home, and I knew it at my core. California was where I lived with my wife, Patricia, and our two children, Blythe and Tom. But Scituate would always be my touchstone.

"Pull the car over, will you, Randy? I think Edison and I will walk from here."

"Are you sure, Tom?" Randy asked. "It's pretty dark out there."

I laughed.

"Oh, sorry," he said quickly. "I wasn't thinking."

"Nighttime is my time, Randy—my time and Edison's. We do even better at night."

It was true. I moved much easier with the big dog when night settled over a place. The change in the air as the fog rolled in compressed the sounds, giving them more focus, more clarity.

"What about your bags?" my friend asked.

"Just take them to the house and leave them on the porch. I'll bring them in when I get there. Thanks for the ride." I got out and handed Randy a tip. "Have one on me, pal, or maybe on the old man."

"I'll do that," Randy said. "I'll have one on Porky."

I wondered how many people were having one on Porky that night. He had affected so many lives, though none more than mine.

As the car pulled away, I picked up the dog's harness in my left hand and felt the pulse as he prepared to go to work. "Okay, Edison," I said. "Let's go home." His harness pull was perfect as I followed my friend through the familiar streets. If you watched us, you probably wouldn't pick up on all of the nuances that made our working relationship so special—the pauses when a tree root was going to be underfoot, the subtle movement, left or right, to guide me around an object, the hesitation reminding me to check for an overhanging branch, and the way he stops at curbs with my toes lined up perfectly on the edge. The dog's performance was flawless, and I knew his commitment was love in its perfect form.

We turned right onto Barker Road, and I knew that it was sixty-three yards from that turn to house number seventy-seven.

Seventy-seven Barker Road—the house that had been the most important place in my childhood. My mother and father never sold it, even after they separated. Mom had come to California to live with us; and my father, well, he had lived in a lot of places. But they kept the house, saying it was important for it to be in the family. My sisters and I used it during sum-mers, and the old man had gone home to live out his remaining days in the comfort of its memories.

I climbed the porch and found the key under the mat where it had always been. Opening the front door, I was assaulted by the mustiness of age and neglect. I shivered as I stepped inside, feeling as if I had entered a tomb, a mausoleum to the past. As quickly as I could, I moved around the familiar spaces, opening windows wide to the sea.

All of the furniture was exactly where it had always been, with my rocking chair positioned in the corner next to the upright piano. How many days had my mother sat in that very chair, supervising my practice, making me play Chopin, Beethoven, Bach, and Mozart, while I wanted to play Chuck Berry and Fats Domino? I owe the success of my musical career to my mother. She knew I had talent, and she understood that talent, like everything else, needed discipline. So I practiced, day after day, scale after scale, exercise after exercise.

I sat in the chair, listening to the ebb and flow of the sea pounding on the cliff below. The surf sound was sharper than in California. I suppose, because the bottom of the Atlantic was more rock-strewn, the cannonaded sound was more like small arms fire, rather than an artillery barrage.

I sat and rocked and listened and rocked, allowing memory to sweep over me, mirroring the same ebb and flow of the sea. On impulse, I stood and crossed to my father's liquor cabinet. It was still there—the crystal decanter with just enough sweet-smelling Jameson's Irish Whiskey for a big drink. I poured it gratefully into a Waterford Crystal glass and returned to my seat.

"Here's to you, Da." I raised my glass in toast. *"Slainte!"*

With the first grateful sip, memories began to flood my mind. Some of them were wanted, some of them not. But all of them were remembered with the clarity of this place, of that time.

3 ⁚ EXPELLED

"YOUR CONDUCT IS COMPLETELY UNACCEPTABLE, Mr. Sullivan. Not only did you put your own life and the lives of the other boys at risk with your absurd stunt, you also required the assistance of the United States Coast Guard, embarrassing this institution with all the coverage your escapade has garnered in the press. What in God's name were you thinking?"

I sat in a hard, wooden chair, facing the desk of Dr. Edward J. Waterhouse, Director of the Perkins School for the Blind. As his anger boiled over, his normally cultured Oxford accent was tinged with the cockneyed tones of his boyhood. "If this were your first attempted escape, we might have been more lenient when considering the appropriate punishment for this kind of conduct. But since it is obvious you do not want to be here, I have no alternative but to expel you from this school."

I heard my mother's audible intake of breath from the chair to my right. "You can't expel Tommy, Dr. Waterhouse," she implored, the pleading obvious in her tone. "He needs this place. He needs all of the learning and special skills that only Perkins provides blind children." I felt her lean forward, one of my mother's gestures of empathy and strength, with her eyes begging him to reconsider.

You see, during my years in the lower school, my report cards always said the same thing: "Tommy is brilliant, but he is a daydreamer, a discipline problem, and he cannot seem to maintain any attention on his work. He excels in music, loves new things, and is a born leader."

I suppose all the trouble I caused at Perkins originated from the first time I went there. It was September 10; we all got in the car: my mother, father, and me, plus Peggy and Jeane. This was unusual in our family, and what was even more ominous was the complete silence that filled our car during the one-hour ride from Scituate to Watertown.

The guard at the gate was named Fritz. I learned over the years that he was German, and I also came to understand that I didn't like him. "You're von da list?" he asked my father.

"My son is a kindergarten student here, enrolling this year," Da answered.

"Let me see," Fritz said. "Let me see," as if he didn't believe my old man. But there I was on the list of new enrollees—*Thomas J. Sullivan, Jr., five, kindergartener*—it was in black and white.

Perkins's campus is divided into two sections—lower and upper schools. The overall property is approximately thirty acres, and even a blind person could not miss the beauty of the place. Every tree that is indigenous to New England grows and flourishes there. Athletic fields were pristine and green. The buildings stood as sentinels to education with the starkness of their gothic architecture. Everything said *old*, *solid*, *permanent* and, yes, *stiff*. Perkins had been created in the style of a British boys' school, even though it was coed. I was about to learn what it meant to be a new boy in this place.

My father pulled the car into the parking area, and we all got out. The smell of fresh-cut grass and something I learned later was a grape arbor made the air heavy with a pungent sweetness that was pleasant but almost overwhelming.

We entered the administration building. My new shoes echoed down the corridor, overamplified by the high ceilings. In the administration office, three women sat behind a long table. Without extending any real greeting, one of them instructed my parents to fill out the obligatory forms.

Another woman bustled in with quick, short steps and an ebullient personality that was supported by an ample physical presence as she hugged me. "So, you're Tommy Sullivan," she said. "I've been waiting for you. I'm Miss Harrison, your housemother. You will be living in Anagnus Cottage. Michael Anagnus, you know, was the second Director of the Perkins

School for the Blind, and your cottage is named after this great man. I'm sure you'll be happy there. There are so many other little boys and girls for you to meet, and they are all waiting for you, so come with me."

She took my hand in her warm, plump one. Though she was wonderfully kind, something grabbed at the pit of my stomach and made my heart skip a beat. *What is she talking about—living in some place called, A . . . A . . . Anagnus? What is Anagnus? We are just here for the day! I'm going back home, aren't I— with my mother and Da and Peggy and Jeane? Or are we all going to live in this place called Anagnus?*

Finally I found my voice. "Mom, Da, are we moving— leaving Scituate? Are we all going to live here in, A . . . A . . . Anagnus?"

"Come on, Tommy," my Da said, avoiding the subject. "Walk with Miss Harrison."

We all crossed what Miss Harrison called the quadrangle or courtyard. "All the cottages face the courtyard," she said. "The classroom building is in the middle, and each cottage has a back-door that leads out onto the athletic fields and playground."

We passed other families moving into their cottages.

"Along with Anagnus," Miss Harrison went on, "there's Bradley, Potter, and Glover, where the girl students live."

Girls? I registered. *I don't want to go to school with any girls!*

As we entered Anagnus, there was a cacophony of sound. Some child was playing the piano. Others had toys out and were on the floor in what Miss Harrison told us was the playroom.

Still others were upstairs, Miss Harrison explained, getting settled. But why did I hear children crying and people saying, "It'll be all right, everything will be all right"? What was all this about?

Miss Harrison showed us the dining room, a pleasant place with big, round tables where she said we all ate together. She even showed us the kitchen where I met the cook, Miss Green, a huge Irish woman who told me that she could make the best cookies in the world. She quickly proved that was the truth when she gave me two chocolate-chip cookies, fresh out of the oven, along with a cold glass of milk. Now that was pretty great, and it temporarily soothed my anxiety.

Then we went upstairs, and everything changed. "Your room will be number eight, Tommy," Miss Harrison said. "Now put your hand on the wall and count with me out loud eight doors."

Hesitantly, I did what she asked. "Five, six, seven, eight," I counted.

"Turn the knob and go in," she said. "Your roommates, Ernie and Jerry, are already there.

Roommates? What does that mean? I thought. Opening the door, I heard a little boy crying. Miss Harrison went to him. "It's all right, Jerry," she said soothingly. "I have someone special for you to meet. Tommy, come here and meet Jerry Pierce."

I followed Miss Harrison's voice and came to the end of— what was it—a bed? Obviously with someone sitting on it. "Jerry," Miss Harrison said, "stand up and shake hands with your new roommate. This is Tommy Sullivan."

One chubby hand replaced another.

"Hi, Jerry," I said. "Are you okay?"

"No," Jerry whined. "I want my mummy. I want my daddy."

"Now, Jerry," Miss Harrison put in quickly. "Remember, I told you that you'll be back home before you know it."

"That's not true!" another voice piped in from across the room. "You told us we won't be going home for one month. That's thirty days, and that's a long time."

"Ernie Anderson," Miss Harrison said, "come over here and meet your new friend, Tommy."

A little boy crossed the room and said rather formally, "Hello. I'm Ernest Anderson. Who are you?"

"I'm Tommy Sullivan," I said, shaking his hand. "I'm glad to meet you."

Jerry was crying again, and pretty soon I understood why.

"This is your bureau, Tommy," Miss Harrison said. "And, let's see, here's the closet, and you have all this space on the right-hand side for your clothes. So let's get you unpacked."

Da produced my suitcase and placed it on the bed that was to be mine. It was in the middle, between Jerry and Ernie. The mattress made a funny sound as my father put the bag on top. I later learned that the mattresses at Perkins were filled with straw and made by adult blind people in a state workshop.

My mother busied herself, helping Miss Harrison unpack my clothes, while my sisters stood quietly in the corner. My jackets and pants were hung neatly in the closet. My socks, underwear, and T-shirts, along with my jeans, went into the bureau drawers. "Your socks are in the top drawer," my mother said. "Your underwear is in the second one. Your T-shirts and jeans are in the third drawer. Now, when your clothes are dirty, just put them in the fourth drawer at the bottom of the bureau until it's time to wash them in the school laundry."

My unpacking complete, an awkward quiet fell over the room, interrupted only by Jerry's sniffling. My Da hugged me hard and kissed me on both cheeks but didn't say anything. The next minute, I heard his feet walk out the door and down the hall.

"Da?" I called. "Da? Where are you going?"

He kept walking.

Then my sisters kissed me and backed away.

My mother was the last of family to hug me. Her tears stung my face as she almost smothered me in her embrace. "I love you, Tommy," she said. "I love you more than anything in the world. I know this is the right thing to do. I know you'll be happy here, Tommy. Tell me you'll be happy here."

Finally I understood what was about to happen. "Don't leave me here, Mummy," I cried. "Don't leave me here!" I clung to my mother, jumping into her arms, wrapping my legs around her waist. "Don't leave me here!"

Miss Harrison began to pull my arms away from my mother and unwind my legs. I screamed and kicked at this fat monster. "No!" I screamed. "No! I won't stay here! I won't stay here! No!"

"It's all right, Tommy. It's all right!" my mother said through her own tears, helping Miss Harrison pry my arms away from her. "I've prayed about this, Tommy, and I know God believes it's all right!"

Now my mother's shoes clicked on the floor as she, too, backed away from me, allowing Miss Harrison to take control of my body. I kicked and screamed, kicked and screamed. "No! No! I won't stay here. I wanna go home. Mom! Da! Don't leave me here. Don't leave me!"

But they were gone—all of them—and I was alone. All alone, sitting on the straw mattress of the middle bed in a room with two strange boys, in a place I hated with all my might. In the memory of my childhood, this separation from my family was the single most difficult experience of my early life. Though Ernie and Jerry became my treasured friends, living in a boarding school isolated from the outside world might as well have been a prison sentence without the possibility of parole. Although my parents believed it was the best thing for their little blind child, placing a five-year-old boy in a school away from home was damaging and impossibly difficult on everyone.

I would return home every other weekend during my years at Perkins, and this led to a confusion of identity that took forever to solve. Was I Tommy Sullivan, a kid locked up in the confines of the Perkins Institute for the Blind? Or was I Tommy Sullivan, a little boy who wanted more than anything to understand the limitless possibilities of the world outside the iron gates?

"Hey, Tommy," Ernie said to me, once I stopped crying. "Wanna go downstairs to the playroom? They've got a lot of good toys down there—blocks and trucks—and Miss Harrison said that someone is going to come and read us stories. Do you wanna go with me, Tommy?"

"No," I said, sniffling. "I just wanna go home."

"Me, too," Jerry said. "Me, too. I just wanna go home, too."

"Well, I'm gonna go downstairs to the playroom," Ernie said. "I'm just gonna go play."

Somehow, the definition of his statement got through to both of us.

"Okay," Jerry sniffed, "I'll go. Come on, Tommy—you come, too."

I decided to go with these two new friends. I guess the necessity of our loneliness brought us together, and before I knew it I was making my way down the stairs to the playroom where I met twenty-six other children my age. We were all the same: all alone, all beginning a new life, all wanting to go home. And for all of us, it was the first day of our adventure in the dark. Jerry, Ernie, and I had many adventures throughout our years at the lower school. One of the most memorable included Miss Green's "world famous" cookies, a temptation we couldn't resist regardless of the consequences.

Jerry, Ernie, and I had snuck down to the kitchen late one night to see if we could swipe a midnight snack. We had learned where Miss Green kept the cookies, and I loved them, not only when they first came out of the oven but also when they had been in the refrigerator and had that cold hardness that felt great to crunch and chew. Our housemaster, Mr. Bartholomew, caught us in the kitchen with our hands literally in the cookie jar, and we were told to go see the director, Dr. Waterhouse, the next morning.

When we reported to the office, we immediately understood that something important was happening. Everyone was working in a hushed manner and seemed to be focused on the front door of the school. *What is happening?* I wondered while I waited to be disciplined by Dr. Waterhouse. I quickly found out the answer. An entourage of visitors came to the office, and I was told to be very quiet because we had a special person coming to the campus.

Perkins had decided to honor its most famous alumnus, the remarkable Helen Keller, on her eightieth birthday. There would be a major ceremony later that day. The press and people from all over the world would attend, and right then Miss Keller was arriving with her teacher and a few other people.

So there we were—Ernie, Jerry, and me—right in the middle of the hubbub. Helen Keller had not only learned to read sign language using the manual alphabet spelled out in her hand, but she had also been the first person to use vibration to disseminate language. By placing her thumb on a person's throat, her index finger on the lips, and her third finger on the bridge of the nose, Miss Keller actually, through vibrations, could understand human speech and then speak in her own voice, an incredible sound that was most peculiar and wonderful.

Her teacher must have told her about the three little boys who were in trouble, because I was surprised when the great lady said to me, "Little boy, they tell me you're a devil. Is that right, little boy?"

I answered, "Yes, ma'am."

I was even more surprised by what she said next. "Good," she said. "Keep it up! Don't ever change. That's how you'll succeed in life. A little devil in all of us," she went on, "brings out the goodness within."

It took me years of trial and punishment to really understand the importance of what Helen Keller had told me, years in which I had taxed the patience of every teacher and frustrated my parents to no end with my desire for freedom. But I believed Helen Keller that day, and I lived my life with her words of wisdom as my guiding light.

Unfortunately, at this moment the head master did not esteem "the little devil in me" like Helen Keller did. "I'm sorry, Mrs. Sullivan," he said. "But Thomas has become a complete distraction to the other students. It is obvious to me that he does not want to continue his education here at Perkins."

"Yeah," I piped in. "I don't want to be here."

I felt my mother's fingers digging deep into my forearm, nearly drawing blood. "Be quiet, Tommy," she said. "We're not talking to you right now."

The voice from the window on the far side of the room seemed distant and surreal. My father's Irish brogue stroked the air in a rather wistful tone. "It's a lovely river out there, the Charles—the way it flows—much like the Shannon, but not as clean. Too bad. I believe salmon would do very well if man wasn't polluting the waters."

He paused, still at the window, and then continued. "I escaped once. Had my own adventure. Left my little village and made it all the way to Dublin before they caught me."

Forty-five years later, the picture of my father is still etched in my mind. Everything about him said raw, masculine power. He was a contrast of emotions. His laugh—a most wonderful sound—was contagious, as if he wanted to share the joke with the whole world. When he was angry, though the brogue still remained, his voice took on a timbre like velvet thunder. There was a menace about my Da—a danger that seemed to always lurk just beneath the surface of his Irish charm.

I heard my mother turn in his direction and knew instantly that she was upset. "Porky, what are you talking about? We don't need to hear a story about your childhood."

"Oh yes, we do, Marie," my father replied evenly, crossing to the desk in two long strides. "Because what we're discussing here, I believe, is Tommy's desire to be a boy, with all its joyous complications. You understand that, don't you, Dr. Waterhouse?"

Now my father was standing, or rather, looming right behind the director's chair. "You understand that my Tommy just wants to be a little boy like other little boys and that this escapade, as you called it, is his way of being part of the world—the real world that's out there, beyond the river."

I sensed a change in the room. The power base had shifted, and my father's aura had become dominant. Director Waterhouse fought to regain control. "There are damages, Mr. Sullivan."

"Oh, you mean the boat, the hole in the fence, and the padlock and chain. I'm sure that a sizable donation to the school will fix all that." My father reached into his pocket, and I heard him take out the wad of bills he always carried, wrapped in elastic. Slowly—very slowly—he began to peel them off, one at a time.

"Let me see. Let me see," he said. "Would this be enough?"

"Porky, stop," my mother broke in, her voice cutting the air like a knife. "Offering Director Waterhouse money is totally inappropriate. We're talking about Tommy's future here."

I heard the sound of my father's smile. "Inappropriate, Marie? Certainly not. You see, in the real world that Dr. Waterhouse lives in and that Tommy wants to be a part of, everything has a price, doesn't it Dr. Waterhouse?"

I listened as more bills were shuffled from the wad.

"Put the money away, Thomas!"

Even my father knew to back off when my mother sounded like that. He sighed, "As you wish, Marie. As you wish."

My mother turned back to the director. "Please, Dr. Waterhouse, I promise we will keep up with all of Tom's school work. Couldn't you just suspend him for the rest of the term and readmit him next fall? That's all I ask. Just give him one more chance."

It was fortunate that Director Waterhouse had an ego bigger than the office we were in. The chance to be magnanimous was exactly what this guy wanted. It was how he liked to think of himself. He allowed a smile as he spoke to my mother.

"All right, Mrs. Sullivan, we'll see. For today, let's call it a suspension. Take Tommy home, and we'll consider his case at some point before the start of the next term. That's the best I can do."

My mother's relief was obvious. "Thank you, Dr. Waterhouse, thank you," she said. "I promise you, nothing like this will ever happen again. Will it, Tommy?" The fingers were back on my arm. "Will it, Tommy?" she repeated, cold steel in her tone. I was daydreaming.

"No, Mom," I said, grudgingly. "Nothing like this will ever happen again." *Until next time*, I thought. *Until next time.*

After this tense meeting we all walked to my father's brand new Oldsmobile Delta 88 with that special new car smell still hanging all over it. Leather seats and a cushy, big car ride. Wow! It was special, and normally I would have loved it—but not today. My mother and father weren't talking, and I figured I better keep quiet.

But inside, I was pretty pleased with the way things had turned out. I mean, I wasn't going to have to go back to Perkins, at least in the near future. And at home, there was my dog, Pal, to play with. Best of all, this afternoon was the opening of baseball season at Fenway Park, with the Red Sox playing their dreaded enemy, the New York Yankees.

As I often did, I leaned forward and turned on the radio, figuring that maybe music would break the silence. "Turn it off," my mother commanded from the back seat. "And stop rocking."

It's a common trait of blind children to rock back and forth whenever they're sitting down. I think it's our way of reducing emotional tension and controlling our nerves. And in my present situation, my eleven-year-old nerves were stretched to the breaking point.

My father finally spoke up. "Now, why are you yelling at the boy, Marie? Hasn't he been through enough, being kicked out of school and all?"

Uh-oh. My mother snapped. "You don't see it at all, do you, Porky? You don't understand that Tommy may never get the education he needs if he doesn't return to Perkins. Public schools are just not equipped to provide blind children with the things they need, and without an education, he could be on the street with a dog and a cup. Is that what you want for your son?"

To my mother education was the key, and her dedication to it was unflinching. I suppose she had good reason, too. For as much as I hated my prison, it offered so much of what my mother dreamed for me: discipline, opportunity, knowledge, and friends. But it hadn't always been seen as the paramount institution of specialized teaching for the disabled. The Perkins School for the Blind was incorporated under the Massachusetts Legislature in 1829 as the Perkins *Asylum* for the Blind. No term has ever been more inappropriate, and no school has ever been more meaningful to the development, evolution, and education of blind people throughout the world. Today, Perkins runs programs for blind children and their families in over sixty countries. Its alumni, such as Helen Keller, have gone on to change the stereotypes connected to blindness around the globe.

All that being said, my matriculation at Perkins in 1952 when I was five years old was a wrenching and painful experience.

My first awareness of what was about to happen to me was not ominous. Actually, it was quite pleasant. A woman named

Miss Kelly came to our house. My mother told me that she was a social worker—whatever that meant—and that she wanted to meet me and decide if I was the right kind of little boy to attend the Perkins School.

The day Miss Kelly was going to arrive, my mother washed my head until my scalp tingled. I was all clean, spit-and-polished in a new shirt and pants and shoes that were stiff because we'd just bought them the day before. All in all, it was a pretty tense time around the Sullivan house. I could feel how seriously my mother took this interview and how much it mattered to her that I be a perfect little boy.

What I remember most about Miss Kelly was that she never spoke to me directly. True, I was only five years old, but she kept saying things like, "Now, I know we will be very happy at Perkins, won't we?" or "You understand, Mrs. Sullivan, we must have Tommy work hard if we're going to succeed in the world of the sighted."

I must've come through okay, because the next thing I knew, my mother and I had to go shopping to find all the right clothes for my Perkins experience. It was required that I have two blazers, four pairs of slacks, white shirts with stiff collars, and either bowties or little clip-on ties developed so that little boys could be even more uncomfortable.

Days started early at Perkins, even for five year olds. An electric bell rang at 6:30 a.m., and our house-parents would go from room to room helping us to get washed and dressed over the next thirty minutes. Breakfast was promptly at seven, and boy, it was quite an event. Imagine how complicated it was to help thirty blind five-year-olds eat their breakfast without spilling stuff all over the place.

After breakfast, we all returned to our rooms to learn basic life skills. We had to learn to make our beds, down to creating hospital corners with the spread at the bottom end. We were also given dust mops and took turns pushing the dirt around the room. We didn't really understand how to pile it into one place, but I guess the cleanliness exercise was a good one.

At eight o'clock another bell would ring, and we'd troop downstairs and across the courtyard to the academic building. Here we gathered with students from the adjoining cottages, so there were about 125 of us, ranging in age from kindergarten through sixth grade. In the seventh grade, students moved to the upper school on the other side of the campus.

Our classrooms were typical. Every student had a desk and learned to put away all his or her school supplies very carefully. Classes consisted of eight to ten students, and my first teacher was Mrs. McGowan.

In today's vernacular, Mrs. McGowan was awesome—a remarkably enthusiastic woman with a great feel for the intimacy necessary to teach blind children. She had a love for each of us that we felt deeply. In time I even learned to like school whenever I was in her presence. She taught us to sing songs as we worked, and she always had a special story to tell or a reinforcing hug to give.

Right from the beginning, we learned about numbers

through the use of the abacus. Each of us had one, and it was fun to move the beads around in columns, divining the mysteries of addition, subtraction, multiplication, and division. Mrs. McGowan also made sure that we learned to do our sums in our heads, a skill that has proven useful my whole life.

We spent a lot of time developing handicraft skills. When I was just seven, I knew how to knit and purl. (Fifty years later, I still have a couple of those old potholders. My wife, Patty, laughs whenever she uses one.) The techniques we learned through handicrafts were useful in other areas, such as tying our shoes. And by working with the sticky dough, we developed a creative sense of what things looked like: animals, people, houses, trucks, or anything else we could think of to build.

Mrs. McGowan taught us to write—or rather, print—our names. She believed that, without a signature, a blind person could never take his place in the sighted world. She probably was the first person to develop a wood block with spaces that allowed blind kids to move the pen straight across the page making our signatures legible.

Braille was our principle form of reading, writing, and learning. Frenchman Louis Braille developed this writing system for the blind in the mid-1800s. Conceptually, it's based on combinations of raised dots to represent letters and numbers read by running the fingers across a page. Each character "cell" is created with a sharp object called a stylus, or with a machine called the Perkins Brailler. So, for example, using the Braille writer and pushing the number one key, you create the letter A. If you press the one and two keys together, you create B. One and four becomes C. One, four, five is D, and one and five pushed together creates the letter E and so on. The key to Braille is developing the tactile sensitivity necessary to move the fingers quickly back and forth across each page.

In later years, my wonderful English teacher, Tony Ackerman, would read Shakespeare to us aloud, his hands moving so fast you could literally hear his fingers on the page from the back of the room. However, in these early days I found Braille to be painful and difficult to learn. My first primer was called *Bob and Kay*. After we learned the letters on playing cards, we began to try to put them together in words and sentences.

The first page of *Bob and Kay* still rings in my memory

Bob and Kay sing,

"Come Bob. Come Kay.

Come and sing.

Bob can sing, and Kay can sing.

Sing, sing, sing."

This memory is indelible because each word took me forever to feel with my fingers and translate in my mind. Reciting to Mrs. McGowan was like toiling painfully, step by step, up some impossible mountain climb.

My friends Ernie and Jerry were much better Braille readers. In fact, everyone in the class was better than I was. I guess I made up for it when we played musical instruments or sang in the Perkins choir. There, I shined. I loved our chorus. Even in the children's choir, made up of all of us from kindergarten through sixth grade, the accuracy of our pitch was fantastic. I learned later that a lot of us had "perfect pitch": we could sing every note on the scale by name without first hearing each note on a piano or other instrument. Consequently, the Perkins choir could learn and perform incredibly complex pieces of music. I remember even in the fourth grade singing the Brahms Requiem, the Mozart Mass, or even Aaron Copland's complex "Stomp Your Foot." Perkins is renowned for its choirs, and it should be.

I also excelled on the playground and athletic field. The Perkins playground was a cool place, with most of the equipment designed for blind kids to use easily. The jungle gym was a maze of bars to climb and go in and out of, with a ladder on the side that led up to a trapeze that I learned to hang upside-down on. There was "The Rocking Boat," a board about fifteen feet long strung between two sets of chains. Kids would lie on their stomachs with four other kids standing at the ends, using their arms and legs to pump the swing to dizzying heights. It was awesome to get this big thing going. To any five-year-old the Giant Swing would be exhilarating, but it was especially so for us at Perkins.

Twenty kids could fit inside "The Rocking Boat," rocking back and forth violently to create a terrific ride in space. There was a ramp with railings on each side padded with foam rubber that in the winter was our sliding hill. It was great to be able to take a sled and independently roar down the ramp, kept in a straight line by the side bumpers.

We had wagons and bikes, a playhouse, and, for me most importantly, a baseball field. We bounced a large ball in front of home plate, where it was hit by the batter. I loved the feeling of contact and then the joy of running the bases. The field had raised cement lines for us to follow with our feet so that we could move around from home plate to first, second, third, and then back again with a homer you'd hit out of the park.

Despite all the wonderful play things and influential teachers I had at the younger school, my rebellious approach to childhood developed the more I longed to go beyond the safe, predictable world of the isolated school. Don't get me wrong, Perkins occupied me for a time. But I knew I was made for more than swings and sledding. I was determined to find out exactly what I was made for, what I could handle. Being expelled proved that I had gone too far (at least in the school's estimation).

My mother was livid, and I had given up on trying to diffuse the tension in the car. Then Da turned to look at my mother. "Listen, Marie," he said, searching for a compromise. "I'll go out and get groceries for the house and take the boy with me. While we're driving, we'll have a little talk, just him and me, and straighten things out. What do you say?" My father could always melt my mother's anger with his blarney and gift of gab.

"You'll do that for me, Porky? Really?"

"Of course," my father said, the smile getting even wider.

4 ⠿ THE RED SOX

MY FATHER BELIEVED HE WAS MUSICAL. IN ACTUAL fact, he was nearly tone-deaf, but it never stopped him from expressing himself in song. I think he believed he had the gifts of John McCormick or other great Irish tenors. Anyway, he was always singing or whistling something. As we drove along that day, I came to understand later that the tune he was whistling with absolutely no sense of pitch turned out to be "Take Me Out to the Ball Game."

The drive to the grocery store seemed to be taking much longer than usual, so I asked the question, "Where are we going, Da?"

He didn't answer, but kept whistling. Then he surprised me by asking a question of his own. "What's this business of 'normie' you were talking about, Tommy, when we were in Director Waterhouse's office this morning?"

"It's what we call all the sighted kids that don't go to Perkins. They're the 'normies,' and we're the 'blindies.'"

My father's response was sharp and cutting. "Don't say that."

"Say what?" I stammered.

"Blindy," he growled. "You are not a 'blindy.' You are visually impaired or sightless. Not blind. Not you, Tommy Sullivan. Do you understand me?"

"Yes, sir," I stammered again, feeling my father's intensity.

His huge hand engulfed my wrist. "Do you understand me, Boyo?" he said again, demanding an answer.

"Yes, Da. I understand. I won't ever say 'blindy' anymore."

"Good. Good. Well then," he went on, gaining back a semblance of control, "what does it mean to you to be a—what was it that you called the other kids—a 'normie'?"

"It means I can be like them, do the things they do, go to public school, play with them . . ."

"Be in the world," he added. "Be a part of life."

We drove in silence for a while, and then he began whistling again as he pulled the big Olds into a parking space.

"Can I stay in the car, Da, while you shop? I think it's about time for the Red Sox game on the radio."

"The Red Sox. Ah, that's right, isn't it, Tommy? Today is opening day, with your namesake on the mound, six-foot five-inch Frank Sullivan himself, the hardest throwing right-hander we've seen in Fenway since Ellis Kinder broke in years ago. I think this will be the year they break the 'curse of the bambino.' 'Teddy Ball' still has a few swings left in that old Louisville Slugger of his, and with Jensen and Piersall playing well and that new kid, Frank Malzone, at third, why, it's the World Series or bust. No. I'm sorry. I insist. There'll be no sitting in the car today."

I shrugged as he got out, coming around to my side and opening the door. "Come on, boy, come on. We haven't got time to waste."

Still disappointed, I stepped out and heard the hubbub all around, and then a sound that told me exactly where I was: "Peanuts here! Fresh peanuts in the shell!" the barker cried. "Red Sox programs here. Get your Red Sox programs."

"Red Sox?" I cried. "Da, where are we?"

"Where two men ought to be, boy, Fenway Park on opening day. Now, come on, let's get the tickets." I threw my arms around my father and hugged him. Peanuts, hot dogs, and the Red Sox, what could be better for any boy?

Da bought tickets in what he called "sun bums' alley," the cheap seats in center field, out in the bleachers. But as we moved through the crowd, the sound of the pitchers warming up and batting practice going on seemed to be getting closer, not further away. We walked down the steps, getting nearer and nearer to the action. I felt like I could almost reach out and touch the green grass of the manicured infield, and even put my hands right on home plate. My father had stopped so close to the field, I felt like I was in the game—a player.

"Hey, Ted," he called, "got a minute?"

Ted? Did he mean number nine, "The Splendid Splinter," Ted Williams? My father had always told me they were friends, but I never met the great man.

And then, there he was. "How are ya, Pork Chop?" he boomed. "Got the boy here for opening day, I see. Wonderful."

"You must be Tommy," he said, stepping into the stands and putting a big arm around my shoulders. "A chip off the old block, your dad tells me, a very special little boy."

"He is, Ted, he is," my father pronounced proudly. "Do you think you might hit one out for the lad today?"

Ted Williams said directly to me, "I promise you that when I hit a homerun off Whitey Ford, it's a homer just for you."

I didn't know what to do—laugh, cry, say something? I was so excited.

"Ted, do you know if Tom's in the ballpark?" my father asked.

"You know how he is, Porky," Williams said. "He gets too nervous on opening day. He likes to watch the game on television from the suite in the Statler."

"Oh, I understand, I understand. Then you think his box might be open?"

"Wouldn't hurt to find out," Williams laughed, knowing exactly what my father had in mind.

"Have a good game, Ted," my father said. "And come around for a drink after you blast one out for the boy."

"I'll do that, Porky," the great man said. "See ya later. Enjoy the game, Tommy. I'm playing it for you."

"Come on, Boyo," my father said. "Let's get to our seats."

We didn't go very far. In fact, we only walked about twenty feet, and there we were in Tom Yawkey's personal box. My father had purchased $2.25 tickets in sun bums' alley, but here we were, borrowing the owner's box on opening day in Fenway Park.

"Ladies and Gentlemen," the PA announcer cried, "please rise for our National Anthem."

My father was always extremely reverent at these times, incredibly grateful to be an American citizen making his living—as shady as it was—in a free democracy. As he quietly sang the words along with John Kiley and the big Hammond organ, he was completely out of pitch but wonderfully sincere as he intoned, "O say, does that star-spangled banner yet wave / O'er the land of the free and the home of the brave?"

The crowd roared, and the umpire cried, "Play ball!" And father and son were caught up, bonded in the common delight found in the national pastime. My father described the game even better than the Red Sox' broadcaster, Curt Gowdy, did on my transistor radio. Da was, well, let me say, more colorful.

For example, the Red Sox fell behind in the first inning when Mickey Mantle, the great Yankee center fielder, caught hold of a high fastball out over the plate and drove it to right field over the Red Sox bullpen for a titanic two-run homer. "Oh my God!" my father said. "The bum really got a hold of that one, Tommy. He hit it a country mile. I tell ya, Boyo, that could end up out on Lansdown Street. I don't know what the devil Big Frank had in mind when he threw that one. He might as well have fed it to him on a silver platter. Holy Cow, he knocked the cover off that thing."

Williams walked in the first inning, and when Ted came up in the fourth, he hit the first pitch out of the ballpark but fouled down the right field line. "What a shot, Tommy," my father said. "Old Ted just got around on it too much, or it would've been a tie ball game."

The next pitch, Ford buzzed Williams with a fastball up and in, causing the great man to hit the dirt. "What in God's name are you doing, Whitey?" my father yelled. "Haven't you got the guts to be a man and throw strikes? What's the matter, ya little bum? Are you afraid 'Teddy Ball' might hit one out? Come on—pitch to him, Whitey."

I don't know if Ford heard my father, but with the count one-and-one, he threw a curve that didn't break, hanging right over the plate, and Ted got it all.

"Oh, Tommy, I wish you could see it. It's a thing of beauty," my father yelled. "It's high and deep, soaring into the heavens. It's going, it's going . . ." And as the crowd roared, so did my father. "It's gone! Some sun bum in the bleachers has a souvenir."

As Ted Williams crossed home plate, people have told me he turned to where we were sitting and tipped his hat. History and legend says that Number Nine never tipped his hat to Red Sox fans. For twenty years they had a love-hate relationship, but my father swore that on that day in 1959, the great ballplayer tipped his hat especially to us.

The game ended with the Red Sox winning 4–3. In the course of the nine innings, I ate four hot dogs, two bags of peanuts, and drank two Cokes. I felt sick, but my father said we had to go by the bar on the way home so that he could pay off the boys and collect what he was owed.

Da always made his bookmaking sound like it was just normal business, even though it was completely illegal in the city of Boston. Gambling, for him, was a pastime he felt every man had the right to do, and wasn't making a living the right of every American citizen? "Wasn't that what the framers had in mind," he would say, "when they wrote the Constitution?"

So we went to the bar to collect his winnings. I hated the Dublin Tavern. I could smell the acrid odors of stale beer and cigarette smoke even before Da's manager, Russell, opened the door. The tavern was a long, narrow structure, with the wooden bar running the entire length of the room. My father also owned Sullivan's Steakhouse, a really fine steak and seafood joint that connected to the tavern through swinging doors at the far end.

This was, in every sense, a man's bar—an enclave for some of Boston's finest and most infamous. In their mutual love of convivial conversation, sports, booze, and business opportunities, men rubbed elbows with seemingly no class system. Cops and crooks, politicians and prizefighters, the real and the phonies, all had a place at Porky's bar, and it was my father, a character larger than life, who kept the whole place hopping.

Remember Norm, the guy on the television show *Cheers*

who was greeted in unison whenever he entered Sam Malone's
Boston pub? In my father's case, it wasn't quite that way. It was
more like the court paying tribute to their king.

"Porky!" someone would shout.

"Hey, Pork Chop. How's it going, kid?"

"Good to see ya, Porky. How did they run at Suffolk
Downs today?"

"What do you know about the Robinson-Pender fight? Any
early lines on the Celtics playoffs?"

As he answered their questions, my father moved through
the sea of men with effortless grace, supported by the squeeze
of a shoulder, a slap on the back, handshakes all around, even
an occasional hug. He was in his true element, while I hov-
ered—no, shrank—by the front door. I knew what was coming:
pretty soon, the customers would notice me. There was nothing quite so patronizing or smothering as the effusive behavior
of a bunch of drunks sucking up to the king and his blind son.

It was Joe Malloy, an ex-con who had done time in the big
house for who knows what crime and now occasionally did special jobs for my father, who recognized my presence. "The boy
is here," he sang out. "The special lad. Little Timmy."

I was glad when the group corrected him with a collective
chorus of "Tommy!"

And then the hands arrived—the hugs, the tussling of my
hair, the slaps on the back, even a couple of sloppy kisses—all
tinged with the breath of men and their cups.

"How's the boy? How's school?"

"Did you love the ball game?"

"That was quite a homerun Ted hit. Did you hear it?"

I was a rat in a maze, a deer in the headlights, a bird with a broken wing that couldn't fly to freedom. But my father seemed oblivious to it all as he conducted business, picking up markers and paying off bets with a large wad of cash—all of it with a blarney bravado laced with Jameson's and Guinness.

Soon I was swept up in the crowd—moved through the bar so that everyone could hug or touch, kiss or cuddle their favorite little boy. It was always like this when Da dragged me into the tavern. And as if rehearsed, I eventually arrived with my entourage at the upright piano set in the far corner. The out-of-tune whiskey bucket was older than the building and served mostly as a countertop for mugs of Guinness.

"Play a couple of tunes, boy," Tussy said effusively. "Help your Da keep the customers happy."

"That's a capital idea," my father boomed. "Give 'em 'Wild Colonial Boy,' Tommy, and then maybe a course of 'Danny Boy.' Oh, make 'em cry, Boyo. If they cry, they'll keep drinking, and if they keep drinking, they'll keep paying."

Everybody laughed as I was lifted onto the piano bench by rough hands while my father banged a beer stein down on the piano's top. "He's not singing for nothing boys. Fill his jar. There'll be no free music here—everybody pays. Tommy needs an education."

"Da, do I have to?" I asked, the appeal clear in my voice.

More laughter.

"Oh, don't be shy, Tommy," my father said dismissively. "Give the boys a tune."

And so I did. And the men sang, drank, and cried while they surrounded me in a haze of smoke and alcoholic appreciation.

Eventually we were back in the Oldsmobile, with my father driving drunk all the way home to Scituate. I don't know how we ever made it on some of those nights. God had a plan for my life. But at every swerve, acceleration, and breaking of the big car, I prepared to die. Unable to see the road, I lived in the panic of not knowing. I prayed we'd be stopped by a policeman. But it never happened, and I suppose even if it did, in 1959 my father would just have paid the cop off. I tried to get him to slow down, but he'd tell me to shut up and not worry. He knew these roads like the back of his hand, he'd say.

And then he'd tell me stories about when he first had come to this country—he'd run from the "Staties" and the "Feds" while working as a bootlegger for the Kennedys during Prohibition. "Don't worry about your old Da," he'd say. "You're safe as a bug in a rug, and I'll get you home lickety-split."

It was fast, all right. Every time we had a night like this, he seemed to be trying to break his own speed record. Eventually, we pulled into the driveway of our Scituate home, both of us knowing the toughest part of the night was still ahead of us: facing my mother.

We didn't have to wait long for the storm to break. Before I'd even made it to the front porch and the safety of my bedroom, the front door banged open and my little mother was

right in his face. "Where in God's name have you been, Porky?"
she demanded. "Don't answer that. I can tell by the smell on ya.
And I suppose the groceries are in the trunk?"

"Now, Re," my father said agreeably, slurring a little. "Don't
go getting on your high horse. The boy and I just had a little
R&R to recover from this morning's ordeal."

"Well, did you talk to him and make it clear that you agree
with me and that he will be returning to Perkins in the fall,
after a summer of keeping up with his studies? Did you do
that, Porky?"

"Of course, Marie," my father said. "We talked about all
those things, didn't we, lad?"

"Oh sure, Da. Sure. We had a good talk."

My mother could always tell when I was lying. Maybe it was
because I answered so quickly. "And where did you have this
little conversation, Tommy?" my mother asked. I paused, just a
beat too long. "I said, where did you have this conversation,
Tommy?" my mother asked again.

"All right, all right, Re," my father put in, getting a little angry.
"I took the boy to opening day at Fenway Park."

"You what?" she snapped.

"I took him to the ball game, where every boy should be
when the Red Sox are playing the Yankees."

"Porky," she said, trying to make sense of it. "Your son has
just been kicked out of school, and you reward that kind of
behavior by taking him to a baseball game? What kind of a
father are you?"

Now I heard my father smiling in the dark. "A loving one," he said. "The kind of father who believes that a little understanding and a spoon full of sugar goes a long way to help the lad build character."

"Oh, that's right, Porky. He'll build character—with all of your bar patrons."

Now the gloves were off. "Those patrons, as you put it, Marie, make it possible for you to have this home and all the lovely things in it. Don't ever forget that. It's the money they pay us that keeps us all out of the poorhouse and provides Tommy and Peggy with a secure future. Or have you forgotten that?"

"What *you* forgot, Porky, is that life is going to be much tougher for Tommy than it is for other boys. It's not enough for him to be equal. He has to be better. And better he's going to be.

"So, get to bed, Tommy," she commanded. "Your work begins tomorrow." With that, she turned on her heel and went upstairs, slamming the bedroom door behind her. I heard the lock click into place, and knew that my father would be spending this night on the too-soft couch or in his big La-Z-Boy recliner.

Da laughed quietly. "Well, I guess that's that, Boyo. Now go up to bed. It'll all blow over in the morning."

As I went up the stairs after my mother, I knew that my father was wrong. The storm had just begun for our family.

5 ⸱ MY BACKYARD

THAT SUMMER, MY SISTER JEANE WAS OUT OF the house and had begun her own family. Peggy was five years older than I and had to cope with a brother who was blind and required all kinds of special attention.

Looking back, it must have been very tough to be Peggy, and I didn't make it any easier. I was a spoiled brat with many demands and a bad attitude. On balance, my feelings of frustration were understandable, but not from Peggy's point of view.

That morning, as I sat down at the kitchen table for breakfast, Peggy and my mother were already having what had become standard conversation about why Da wasn't home.

"Your father's working, Peggy," my mother said.

"Oh sure," Peggy replied. "That's why I heard him driving off in the middle of the night."

"Don't be smart, young lady," my mother warned. "We don't need any of your impertinence this morning. Eat your breakfast and get to school."

Peggy shifted the subject, taking on a more conciliatory tone. "Okay, Mom. I'm sorry. Listen, I've got something to talk to you about, and it's very important."

My mother stopped working on preparing breakfast. "Yes? What is it, Peg?"

"Well, I've been asked out on a date for Saturday night—my first real date. And I really want to go."

"Peggy's got a da-ate. Peggy's got a da-ate," I put in.

"Shut up, Tommy," Peggy said. "This is important."

"Peggy's got a da-ate. Peggy's got a da-ate."

"Be quiet, Tommy," my mother said. "You're in enough trouble already, so don't make it any worse." That shut me up.

"So, what do you think, Mom?" Peggy went on. "Do you think it's all right for me to go?"

"Peggy, you know your father and I go out every Saturday night for dinner. It's our one evening to be together, and we need someone to watch Tommy."

"Why does it have to be me?" Peggy asked. "I have plenty of friends. I'll find someone to be with Tommy."

"You're not ready to go out on dates yet, Peggy," my mother said. "Not until you're sixteen. And that's a year away."

"It's always about Tommy," Peggy cried. "Everything is about Tommy. Doesn't anybody ever think about me?"

At that moment, I felt sorry for my sister. I could tell in her voice how much this date meant to her, and the need to be a smart aleck evaporated. "It's okay, Mom," I suggested. "I can stay with a friend of Peg's."

"See, Mom," Peggy said. "Tommy's gonna be okay."

"I'm sorry, Peggy," my mother said, "but you're just not ready for dating." Crying, Peggy ran out of the room. I felt bad for her, but this was not the moment to argue with my mother.

Right on cue, my mother turned back to me. "Tommy," she went on, "if you reach to your right at the end of the table, you'll find all of your schoolbooks put in order."

My hands took in the immense pile of work I was expected to be doing.

"This morning," she continued, "you'll begin reading the biography of Helen Keller. I want you to be inspired by this great woman, and it's a perfect book for your required five-page report for English class."

I wanted to groan, but I knew this wasn't the time.

My mother softened a little, opening the back door. "It's a beautiful spring morning," she told me. "You might want to work outside in the sun. That's a lot better than sitting in a stuffy classroom. So you get to work while I check on your sister."

I remember reading that there are six billion people in the world and that the circumference of the earth is approximately twenty-one thousand miles around. Until the dawning of the automobile and the railroad, travel by foot and on horseback was measured in days, rather than hours. How we view the world depends on how we live in it. For me, the globe stretched out through the power of my imagination.

Books, movies, television, and radio connected me to far-flung destinations and adventures, if only in the mind of a blind child. My real world, however, was mostly confined to my fenced-in backyard. Believing that they were keeping me safe, my parents had fenced in our property with a high chain-link barrier that kept me inside while the world moved inexorably outside. It had been that way for as long as I could remember.

But now, in my eleventh summer, the intense desire to break out—to risk in order to understand—had reached the point of desperation. There was so much I needed to know, so much I wanted to touch and taste, smell and hear. My mind and my senses were alive with all of the possibilities I had read about. And now, on my first morning home after being expelled from Perkins, my desire for freedom was unquenchable. Since I had broken out of prison and felt the excitement of life on the river, it would be impossible to contain my dreams.

And so, when my mother told me to take my books and go outside, I could not keep my mind on anything found in the pages. I wanted to live in the world, not read about it. I craved the excitement I felt on the river after the prison break. Since then, it had been impossible to contain my dreams of freedom.

I went to the old swing in the corner of my yard and sat on it. From the time I was a little boy, that swing had served many purposes. If I sat sideways on its seat, it was the Lone Ranger's stallion, Silver, as I rode chasing Butch Cavendish and the Hole-in-the-Wall Gang. Twisting the chain as taut as possible and then releasing the swing, I was Flash Gordon and the swing became a rocket ship flying through space. At other times, pumping as hard as I could and taking the swing through its complete arc, I was a bird, soaring over the confines of my yard, tasting delicious freedom. While I was on my swing, the sounds of the world came to me on the ocean's breeze, tempting me with unlimited possibilities.

My radio was a critical link to my global experience. It was a big transistor job that took about a zillion batteries to operate. I would bring it outside and set it on the back steps, becoming part of the radio dramas that played until after the sun went down. I was Johnny Dollar, detective extraordinaire. I chased organized crime with The Gangbusters and often became Lamont Cranston, The Shadow, acting as a force of justice against the evildoers.

On rainy days, when I was forced to play inside, I used a variety of sound effects to amplify my fantasies. Curtain rods clanged together made for great sword fighting. Old shoes pounded on the carpet became horses galloping over the prairie. Crackling cellophane was a runaway forest fire as, along with Lassie, I saved wild animals from disaster. In all of these episodes, I was a hero. I suppose in characterizing myself this way, I was searching for a positive sense of self-worth. And I found it in the unlimited capacity of the human imagination.

Spring had dawned in New England. The groundhog must

not have seen his shadow that year because the earth was taking on the richness of new life. From my swing, I could smell
early, fresh-cut grass, along with the headiness of apple blos-
soms and lilac. At the far corner of our yard was a large oak tree
where a robin had placed her nest. The sound of her cheerio
song touched my soul and lifted my spirits.

Just down the street from my house was the neighborhood
public school, along with a beautiful Little League baseball
field. Every day I fantasized that I was part of it all. *Why can't I
be part of that world?* I wondered. I was as smart as the children
I heard moving between classes each time the bell rang, or playing dodge ball during recess. *I could go to public school if I could
just break out of this yard.*

My mother interrupted my reverie. "Tommy," she called.
"It's time for you to come in and work on your piano lesson
until lunch. If you were in school, this would be your fourth
period by now. Have you done any work, or have you just been
sitting out there, daydreaming? Remember, things are going to
be just the way they would be if you were still in Perkins, so
let's get cracking on your music. Young man, it's now time for
the masters. And with the first signs of spring, I think it would
be a wonderful day for Chopin, maybe some of the preludes
you were working on with Mr. Johnson earlier this year."

My mother loved the piano, and though her formal study
was limited, she read music well and played with a passion that
rivaled that of any concert performer. In 1959 my mother urged
me to play Chopin, but I was developing a heavy left hand and

learning to copy Little Richard, Jerry Lee Lewis, and Fats Domino. Mom believed the arts would make the difference in my ability to connect to the world, and said that music would be my ticket out of darkness. In a way she was right, although it was not classical music that made the difference. In later years, it was my ability to play at parties and in bands that helped me to bridge the gap between myself and other young people.

On this spring day, I actually enjoyed playing the Chopin preludes, with my mother helping me along by suggesting better fingering. She surprised me after lunch by telling me that was enough for the day and that I could go back outside to pursue my biggest fantasy, baseball.

I don't know why baseball so captured my attention. Maybe it was the anticipation built into the game as the pitcher winds up and the batter digs in. Maybe it was the hero worship I felt toward Ted Williams, or the fact that my father knew many of the players that frequented the Dublin Tavern and Sullivan Steakhouse. Whatever it was, I lived for the game. And though my Da took me to Fenway Park on special occasions like opening day, most of my connection to the great American game came via the Red Sox broadcast on WHDH 850 on your radio dial. When I made believe I was part of the game, the fence that kept me inside my backyard became the "green monster," left field at Fenway Park.

And this early spring day was no exception. For the second game of the series, the Red Sox were pitching their brilliant left-hander, Mel Parnell, and the Yankees were countering with their own Mel—Mel Stottlemyre. Like all of my play, my baseball was as active as I could make it. Da had bought me an old Louisville Slugger bat, and since I couldn't chase any ball I might have been lucky enough to hit, I was glad that my yard was filled with an abundance of rocks and pebbles.

The object of my game was to follow Kurt Goudy's play-by-play, standing at the end of my yard and throwing rocks up in the air, hoping that if a Red Sox player got a hold of one, I might just do the same. The truth was, not being able to see the rock, I might hit one out of every fifty tries. But those moments, even if the stone only flew just a few feet, was a life highlight to an eleven-year-old blind boy who desperately wanted to be part of the game.

It was the seventh inning and a 2–2 tie when the school bell rang to let all the neighborhood kids out for the day. Every time I heard that bell, I felt a twinge in my stomach. I was lonely, surrounded by activity without being a part of it. Every time that crowd of kids poured out of the building onto my street, I wished for another lonely boy looking for a friend. *There has to be some kid*, I thought, *who needs a friend*. I was so ready to fill that space.

In the meantime, in that spring of 1959, I lived in hopes and dreams, adventures and fantasies. Thank God, most children are wonderful optimists. As I played my make-believe game, I convinced myself that one day I might stand in Fenway Park as a member of the Boston Red Sox. Why not? I already knew Ted Williams.

On the radio, the Red Sox had runners on first and second with two on and two outs as Jim Piersall came up to bat. Piersall was the fiery Red Sox center fielder, and I loved him because he'd do anything to win. It was said that Jimmy Piersall was a guy who'd go into the stands after a fly ball, and I can remember him doing that on a number of occasions. I dug in at my imaginary home plate, hoping that Jimmy and I would both connect and hit one out.

Kurt Goudy set the scene. "So, here we are, BoSox fans, in the last half of the seventh inning in an early season barn-burner with twos across the board: two to two, two outs and two men on and free-swinging Jim Piersall at the plate."

I swished the bat around in the air, making believe I was getting ready.

"Stottlemyre's really had the boys swinging at air today. Yes sir, Ladies and Gentlemen, the 'Junk Man' is throwing up plenty of it. He may not have a ninety-five-mile-an-hour fastball, but with his good slider curve and changeup, the boys are swinging like rusty gates on a farmhouse fence. Mel toes the rubber. Here's the windup and the first pitch to Piersall."

I threw the rock up into the air and swung violently. So did Piersall.

"Strike one," Goudy called. "Oh boy, Jimmy was trying to hit it out to Lansdown Street. Take it easy, Jim, a base hit's as good as a homer. Stottlemyre looks in for the sign, gets it from Yogi. Again, he's into the windup. And here's the pitch."

This time, when I threw the rock up in the air, I purposely didn't swing, and neither did Piersall. Maybe I was a psychic.

"Ball one," Goudy said. "That curveball just broke a little too fine on the outside corner. The count is one ball and one strike. Jensen takes a lead off first. Goodman eases his way off second. Stottlemyre kicks and throws."

At such moments, the forces of nature all seem to come together: a perfect sunset on a blue ocean, a great Bordeaux drunk at the peak of the grape, the chemistry of two people falling deeply and passionately in love. Now this. Was it kismet?

Goudy's voice told the story. "Stottlemyre kicks and throws. It's a high drive."

Bat and ball—and bat and rock—connected at the same instant.

"Deep into center field, Mantle going back to the warning track, back to the wall, looking up. This one is going . . . going . . . Hello! Three-run homer."

I heard the crowd roar through the teeny radio speakers as I took off, running around my yard as if I were running the bases, ecstatic in my accomplishment and totally unaware of being watched by someone with no joy in his soul or kindness in his heart. Eddy Mullins was a bully's bully, one of those rare examples of a kid who was truly mean-spirited. I'm sure some psychologist could figure out why Eddy was like that, but at the time no explanation would justify this bully to an eleven-year-old blind kid. Eddy Mullins nearly ruined my life.

As I rounded my imaginary third base and sprinted toward home plate, crossing it and bowing to the crowd, I was surprised by the voice that cut through my reverie. "What's the matter with you, kid? Are you blind?"

My immediate reaction was, *Wow, maybe a friend.* I was so excited and naïve in my longing that I didn't pick up on the sarcasm in his tone.

"I'm Tom Sullivan," I told him. "And, yeah, I'm blind. Who are you?"

"I'm Eddy Mullins," he said. "And you're not only blind, you're stupid."

I felt the blow of his words right in my gut and wasn't sure how to respond.

"I'm not stupid," I stuttered, "I'm just making up a game."

"Well, it's a stupid game," he said, "played by a blind, stupid kid."

I moved toward the sound of his voice, still hoping . . . I don't know what I was hoping.

"Don't say that. Don't talk to me like that," I told him.

"Okay," he went on, "then I'll just sing you a little song."

It's often said that a person cannot remember pain, that the feeling is lost with time. We remember when we were sick or hurt, but the actual feeling of pain seems to go away with the years. That may be, but when I remember Eddy Mullins' little song, the affect on me is as vivid today as it was in 1959.

"Blindey-Blindey-Blindey," he sang. "Blindey-Blindey-Blindey."

"Don't do that," I said, my anger rising to the surface, tears forming behind my sightless eyes. "Don't say that."

"Blindey-Blindey-Blindey."

"Don't say that!"

"Blindey."

I dropped to the ground, my tears staining the green grass. I scrambled, searching for rocks, and found three.

"Blindey-Blindey-Blindey."

"I hate you," I cried, and threw the first stone, forcing Eddy to duck.

"Ha, ha. You missed me."

The bully was enjoying the game. I hurled the second stone, but now Eddy had moved, and his chant had changed. "You-can't-hit-me. Blindey-Blindey-Blindey."

"I hate you!" I screamed. "I hate you!"

"Blindey-Blindey . . ."

I threw the third stone and heard it harmlessly bounce off a tree.

"I hate you!"

In the background, I heard my father's car pulling into the driveway and the doors slam. "What in the name of all that's holy is going on here?" my Da roared. "What are you doing to my son?" I heard my father starting purposely toward the yard. "What's going on here?"

Eddy's feet beat a quick retreat at the approaching giant. Like all bullies, he was fundamentally a coward. In the next instant, my father had his arm wrapped around my shoulders, hugging me close. "What's the matter, Tommy? What happened here?" he asked.

Now the tears were running full force down my face. "He called me 'Blindey,' Da," I said, shaking. "He called me 'Blindey.'"

My father was quiet, hugging me close. "Remember what I've told you, Tommy," he finally said. "You're not blind. I promise you, you see more than every kid in this neighborhood. We just have to make them understand."

6 : PEGGY'S BLIND DATE

AFTER MY PAINFUL BACKYARD EPISODE, THE REST of my week, frankly, sucked. I sat on my swing feeling worse and worse. And even the world outside my fence didn't seem like such a great place. I couldn't understand how anyone could be so cruel. And the idea that little boys like Eddy Mullins were out there made me wonder if I was better off behind the fence. Maybe my mother was right—maybe blind people needed to be protected. I just didn't know.

By the time Saturday night rolled around, I was in a pretty bad mood. So, who could I pick on? Whose life could I make as miserable as mine, just because I was feeling awful? Why, my big sister Peggy, of course.

Saturday nights were a big deal for my parents. Both of them would get dressed up, and there was always a feeling of excitement and anticipation as my mother primped and got ready. I could hear her humming and singing as she got dressed upstairs. It always took a long time, but when she came down and took my father's arm, I clearly understood that this was a time for them full of love and happiness. "We may be out late," Mom said to Peggy, "but you know the restaurant we are going to."

"And the hotel where we'll be dancing 'til dawn!" my father put in.

My mother actually giggled, "Oh, Porky," she said, coquettishly.

Peggy just nodded sourly. When the door closed, an icy silence immediately gripped the room. Eventually, I couldn't take it. "What should we do, Peg?" I asked. "Watch TV or play monopoly? How about some fish with my Braille cards, or maybe you could read me a story?"

"We're not going to do any of those things," she said coldly. "You're going to do exactly what I tell you to do, or I will make your life miserable."

"Why are you so mad at me, Peggy?" I asked. "I didn't do anything."

"You just exist," she said, "and I always have to take care of you. Do you know what it's like being your older sister and having to babysit you all the time? Take you with me wherever I go? Always have you there when I'm trying to hang out with my friends? It's no fun being your sister, Tommy."

"Well, I don't like being your brother," I protested. "You're always whining and complaining. You're never any fun, and you never let me do anything I really want to do."

"Okay, Tommy," she said, changing her tone, "I'll make a deal with you. If you help me tonight, I'll be nice to you for the rest of my life."

"What?" I asked, surprised.

"You heard me, Tommy. If you help me tonight, I'll be nice to you for the rest of my life. I mean it."

"What do you want me to do?" I asked.

She actually put her arm around me. "I want you to go out with me on a date with Jackie Murphy. We're going to go to a movie, and I'll get all the popcorn and stuff you want to eat if you'll just be quiet and not be a little brat. Will you do that for me, Tommy? Please?"

I thought about how mean Peggy had been to me for so long. I thought about how many times she said she hated me, and then I thought about how much fun it would be to go on this date with my sister. "Okay," I said, smiling. "I'll be nice as pie. You won't even know I'm there."

"Great," she said, running up the stairs. "Let me call Jackie. If we leave in fifteen minutes, we can make the show."

It's amazing how fast a girl can get dressed when she wants to. In about ten minutes, Peggy was back downstairs, humming out loud like my mother and smelling . . . and smelling good! I heard Jackie's car coming down the street at least a minute and a half before he pulled into our driveway. I don't know what kind of souped-up hot rod he owned, but it was loud.

We roared off to the drive-in with me in the back seat and Jackie and Peg up front, blasting the radio and talking quietly so I couldn't hear them above songs from The Drifters and The Platters, all brought to us by Wolfman Jack, one of the first great rock-and-roll deejays.

The drive-in—a phenomenon of the fifties—was a place where, for less than a buck, you could pull into a parking space, stick a small speaker through your window, go to the Snack Shack and buy all of the junk food you could handle, and watch a triple. If you got there right at sunset, you could see some kind of low-budget B movie, usually something like *The Monster That Devoured Cleveland*, followed by two cartoons and then, hopefully, some kind of a steamy main feature that enabled American teens to enjoy some heavy necking in the back seats of jalopies and hot rods all over the country. Drive-ins were considered "passion pits," and that's why the Catholic League considered it a mortal sin if kids like Peggy and me went there. Tonight Peggy and Jackie got real lucky. The main feature, *Peyton Place,* was so steamy my mother would have been shocked to know Peggy was seeing it.

"So, what would you like to eat, Tommy?" Peggy asked, more solicitous than I could remember her being in a long time. "They have everything here." I put in an order for a large bag of M&M's, two Hershey Bars, a large popcorn, and a vanilla Coke, thinking I'd top it all off later with an ice-cream sandwich.

What a night. Peggy sent Jackie to get my food. She then turned to me, becoming even sweeter, if that were possible. "Tommy," she said, "when Jackie comes back, we're going to change places. I want you to sit up in front, and Jackie and I will sit in the back so that we can see the screen better." She laughed. "You don't have to see the screen, do you, Tommy?"

I wasn't that stupid. I didn't know exactly what they did in the back seat of cars like Jackie's, but I understood from movies on television that kissing and stuff was going on. And I also understood that she didn't want me to get in the way. What a magnificent opportunity to really give my sister the business— to pay her back for all the rotten things she did to me. I was going to make her very sorry she had brought me along on her drive-in date. Oh boy! This was going to be great!

Jackie came back with all the food, and we made the switch. His car was a two-door, so we all had to get out. Then Peggy and Jackie climbed in the back, and I climbed in front. "Now, push your seat up a little bit, will you, Tommy?" Peggy asked, still saccharin-sweet.

I found the lever and gave them a few more inches.

"Thank you, Tommy. Now, enjoy your food. Here comes the first feature. I know you'll love it. It's called *Godzilla*."

The bad theme music warbled through the speaker attached to the window on my side of Jackie's car. Peggy leaned forward and turned the sound up all the way, figuring I wouldn't hear what was going on in the back seat. Poor, poor girl! She didn't understand that blind people can hear *everything!*

So, when ol' Jackie moved over and put his arm around my sister, I heard every bit of the slimy slide, and as Godzilla appeared for the very first time, and Jackie and my sister started to kiss, or rather "suck face," I piped right up. "Peggy, Peggy!" I

said. "What's happening? The monster, I mean. What's happening, Peggy?!"

The kiss abruptly stopped.

"The monster is coming into the city," she told me, a tinge
of irritation in her voice. "Now, go back to your candy and don't
bother me. I'll tell you about the whole movie during intermis-
sion. Okay, Tommy?"

"Okay," I said, loving every minute of the interruption.

As the monster continued to work on destroying Tokyo,
Jackie worked on moving in on my sister. The next time he
went for the big make out, I let him have a minute or so to get
really into it, and then said with pain in my voice, "I'm feeling
sick! I think I'm going to throw up."

"You're not sick," Peggy said, really angry now. "Just take a
few deep breaths and watch the movie and shut up."

"I am too sick! I'm going to throw up right now!"

"No!" Jackie cried. "Not in my car. Don't throw up in my car."

I made a retching sound, like I was going to barf.

"No!" he cried, pushing the seat on the driver's side forward
and throwing open the door. He literally leapt over Peggy, and
I think he must have kicked her in the head because she sort of
yelled. Then Jackie was pulling me out the driver's door as I
kept making those throw up sounds. It was all really cool.

They both walked me around for a while, and, of course, I
didn't throw up. I told them the air was making me feel better.
Eventually, we went back to the car just as the cartoons started.
Jackie and Peggy were having an argument.

This is even better than I expected.

"Forget him, Jackie," Peggy was saying. "Don't let the little brat spoil our night. Let's make out."

Timing is everything.

"I have to go to the bathroom," I said, "really bad!"

"Just hold it," Peggy nearly screamed.

"I think I'm gonna pee in my pants. I'm gonna pee in my pants."

"That's it," Jackie said, getting out of the driver's side again. "I'm taking you home."

"No, Jackie." Peggy was crying now. "Don't listen to him!"

"I'm gonna pee in my pants. Really. I am, right now."

Jackie was in the driver's seat, starting up the car and disturbing all the other movie patrons. You could hear them yell at him. "Hey, turn off the motor." "We're trying to watch the movie." "Turn off that loud piece of crap."

Peggy was still pleading, "Jackie, we don't have to go home. Really, we don't. I'll get him to shut up, I will!"

"We're going," Jackie said, letting off the emergency brake.

"I don't think you want to drive yet," I put in.

"Shut up," he said.

"Okay, but don't say I didn't warn you."

Jackie put the car in gear and peeled rubber out of his parking space—a serious mistake. The heavy, metal speaker was still attached to his front window, and as he roared away the speaker broke the glass and snapped his window right out of its track. The crash was wonderful.

Now Jackie was actually crying. As for Peggy—well, Peggy was embarrassed and angry. Without question, in that magnificent moment she hated me as much as it was possible for a sister to hate a brother.

When we got home, she dragged me into the house. "Listen," she hissed. "If it's the last thing I ever do, I'll get back at you for this, Tommy. Somehow, someway, I'll pay you back!" She ran up the stairs, slamming her bedroom door, crying with hurt and rage.

And what did I do? Well, I found some milk and cookies in the kitchen, feeling like I oughta top off all the other junk food I had eaten, and then settled down in Da's big chair to watch a little television on a perfect Saturday night.

A few days later, Peggy took her revenge. I was downstairs having breakfast when my sister showed up smelling good again. Peggy was a typical fifteen-year-old who never got out of bed before eleven or twelve o'clock unless my mother went upstairs and yelled at her. I don't know how anybody could stay in bed so long, but Peggy seemed to do it all the time. So why was she down here for breakfast at eight? My mother also registered the surprise.

"Good morning, Peggy," she said cheerfully. "Will miracles never cease? Except for when you are in school, I don't know when I've ever seen you up at this hour of the day. What's so important that you've chosen to join us?"

"Oh, I was going to the beach to meet some friends early this morning," Peggy said, "and I thought maybe you'd like me to take Tommy."

What? I thought. *She hates to take me to the beach. Now she wants me to go? Something's weird.*

"Peggy, that's very kind of you," my mother said. "I do have a lot of work to do around the house, so it would be great if Tommy could spend the morning with you. You'd like that, wouldn't you, Tommy?"

Only if I can swim, I thought. A lot of times when Peggy would take me to the beach, I'd have to just sit in the sand while she gabbed with her friends, bored out of my mind. I decided to try and get my mother on my side.

"I don't wanna go," I said. "All we ever do is hang around with her friends and sit on the sand. I never get to swim or anything."

Peggy went back to sweet. "We'll take you in the water today, Tommy," she said. "It's really hot out, and everybody will want to swim, so there will be plenty of people to play with you."

"Sounds great!" my mother said, probably relieved that she didn't have to take care of me for the day. "Just don't go out too far or go in the water right after you eat. You know, that's when people get those horrible cramps."

Peggy was probably hoping I'd get one.

Anyway, twenty minutes later with towels over our shoulders, we headed for Sand Hills Beach. As we walked along, Peggy asked conspiratorially, "Would you like to do something really fun today, Tommy?"

"Like what?" I asked, figuring Peggy had an ulterior motive.

"Like, go out on a boat," she said, excited.

"Sure," I said. "I love boats."

She went on enthusiastically, "Jackie owns a speedboat! It's really fast and really cool. Instead of just going to the beach, you and I can go cruising. What do you think, Tommy?"

She had me hooked! "That'd be great, Peg. Let's go!"

So when we got to the beach, Jackie pulled his boat right up on the sand, and minutes later we were roaring across the bay. What a feeling. I had never gone this fast before, and the boat seemed to be flying over the waves. It was like a ride at an amusement park, with that just-a-little-bit-scared feeling in the pit of my stomach.

The thing was, Jackie was being nice to me. He even let me hold the wheel and steer the boat while he told me which way to turn. It felt like he really liked me.

Then, somewhere out in the open ocean, things began to change. "Oh my God!" Peggy cried, acting her part very well. "You can't believe it, Tommy. I've never seen anything like this before."

"What, Peggy?" I asked. "What are you talking about?"

"Sharks," she said. "A whole school of sharks. You can see their fins just above the surface of the water."

Jackie brought the boat to a stop, and we drifted. Peggy went on. "Maybe you can hear them swimming, Tommy? Oh wow. They are all around our boat."

I bent my head down, close to the rail, listening. I couldn't hear anything, but my imagination took over, and I believed I did.

"What do they look like, Peggy?" I asked.

"They're long and sleek," she said, "with gray fins sticking up just out of the water, and when they swim, they seem to glide.

WHOA! One just went right under the boat! Here he comes again. Listen, Tommy. See if you can hear 'em."

I was sure I did!

Then Peggy's tone changed. "Remember the drive-in, Tommy?" she said. "Remember how you made believe you had to throw up, and then you made believe you had to go to the bathroom, and you kept talking, ruining my whole night? Do you remember all that, Tommy—what a little brat you were? Well, this is when *we* get even."

All at once, Jackie and Peggy grabbed me, and before I even had a chance to yell, they threw me over the side. "Come on, sharks," Peggy called, "here's your lunch."

Jackie put the boat back in gear and they drove off, leaving me alone in the ocean, screaming. During earlier summers in Scituate, I had taken swimming lessons, and so drowning wasn't an issue, but the panic I was feeling—waiting for the sharks to bite—cannot be described. What would the big fish take first? My legs? My arms? I didn't know as I waited for the first big bite. But it never came, and minutes later Peggy and Jackie drove back and picked me up, laughing.

I was shaking. "I hate you!" I said to Peggy. "I hate you!"

"That's okay," she said, enjoying the moment completely. "I hate you, too."

I thought about telling our mother about what Peggy had done, but then I figured that would just keep the war going, and maybe in the end I wouldn't win. So, an uneasy truce seemed to settle between us. We didn't talk. We just coexisted.

Several weeks after this happened, it was another Saturday night, and my parents were out. I watched television until Peggy told me I had to go to bed.

I don't know how long I'd been asleep when the dreams started. I was back in the ocean alone, and the sharks were attacking. First they circled me, bumping me as they swam by. I could hear their teeth snap close by my face, but I was paralyzed, unable to move or scream. In my dream I didn't feel pain, but I knew every detail of what was happening to me.

The first shark took my left arm, and I could taste my own blood in the water. The next one grabbed me below the waist. I don't know how much of my legs he got. I could feel my life ebbing away. There would be no more Tom Sullivan—no more hopes and dreams, no more possibilities. This is how I would die, and it was Peggy's fault. She had thrown me in the water.

Another shark was moving in for the kill. I must have screamed because the next thing I knew, someone was there hugging me. "It's all right, Tommy. It's all right. You're all right." As I came awake, I understood that the voice was Peggy's. "It was just a dream, Tommy. It was just a dream."

"Sharks," I said, still crying. "It was the sharks."

Now Peggy was crying, hugging me, rocking me back and forth. "I'm sorry, Tommy," she said. "I'm so sorry. I never should have done anything like that to you. I know you're only a little boy, and I love you, Tommy. I love you more than anything in the world. I'd never let anything hurt you. You know that, don't you, Tommy?"

"But you threw me in the ocean. You threw me in the ocean, and there were sharks—big sharks."

"There were no sharks, Tommy. I was just being mean because of what you did to Jackie and me at the drive-in. I'm sorry. I'm so sorry, Tommy."

We stayed that way for a long time, my sister and me, crying and holding each other. Our lives changed that night.

7 : KENTUCKY BLUE

MY FATHER'S PUB WAS THE FAVORITE DRINKING
enclave for his group of Irish cronies, but on Saturday nights
and often well into Sundays it was our house that was the true
seat of the lace-curtain aristocracy.

To gain entrée into Porky's Saturday poker circle meant that
you were a power broker—someone respected and maybe even
feared by your peers. On these remarkable evenings, lions sat
down with lambs. The range of men at the table ran from former governors and the present mayors to police commissioners
and a few highly successful persons from the other side of the
law. It was as if Porky's card table was Switzerland—completely
neutral. The cop might be trying to bust the bookie during the

week, but on Saturday nights at Porky's card games, the business of the week was always put aside.

This oddity arose mostly because all of these men had come
up the hard way, and had suffered the indignity of Boston
Brahmin, descendants of Boston's protestant founders who
hated Irish Catholics. Truth be told, many of them had known
each other since childhood, when they had all scrambled in the
streets, growing up hard and trying to make a buck. I suppose
that's why the crooks could befriend the cops, and the cops
could turn their backs on the illegal activities carried on by their
childhood pals.

As I said, you had to be on Porky's A-list to sit at the table,
which meant you had to have the wherewithal to lose heavily
but not jeopardize your home or family. Porky's basic rule was
that you could empty a guy's pockets, but he had to be able to
pay his mortgage and feed his loved ones.

My father had lost his own dad when he was ten, a life-
changing experience for him, and he had always found a way to
keep a roof over his mother's head. Da had done it all: from
hard labor to taking hard shots in the ring as a professional
prizefighter; from his bookmaking operations to the pubs he
now ran so successfully; and all the way back to the days during
the Great Depression when he worked as a bootlegger for the
infamous Joe Kennedy. My father ran the gauntlet, bringing the
Scotch in from the big supply ships and hiding in small coves
and inlets from the U.S. Coast Guard.

I loved Saturday nights. I could enjoy my father's cronies

and escape to my room whenever I needed to. Before the game would start, I would take a big quilt and an old pillow and find a place to enjoy the night, usually behind the old upright piano where I could remain out of sight and just listen to the talk.

And oh, there was talk. Those special nights the hubbub went from betting blarney to business brokering to B.S., spiced with the most amazing epithets that have ever been strung together over pots won or lost.

My mother hated the swearing. She tried to stop it in the only way she could. "If you're going to be in my house," she'd say, "you'll tack a dollar up on the wall every time you use any of that fowl language. Do you understand me, Captain Michael Murphy of the Boston PD?"

"Yes, ma'am," the captain said, cowering from my mother's steely resolve.

"What do you do with the money you collect from us, Marie?" City councilman Charley Powers asked my mother. "I give it to Catholic charities," she said, "in the hope that a sizable donation might just save your lost soul."

The roar of male laughter pealed off the wall.

"Nothing will save his soul, Marie," Mayor James Donovan put in. "He sold it to the same *divil* that owns the conscience of all us harp politicians. It's much too late, so don't waste your prayers on him."

"Come on, boys, come on," my father said. "We haven't got time for a wake. Let's deal the cards."

They played five-card stud with deuces wild, and you've

never heard so much whining and complaining as chips were slid back and forth across the table, along with heaping plates of food from my mother's kitchen. I often wondered why she slaved to feed these people. Was it her sense of wifely obligation or, in her way, did she enjoy the camaraderie of the men? I'm not sure. But what I do know is that the secret of the game was to be able to keep your wits about you while you drank copious amounts of whiskey, beer, and Guinness.

My father was one of the first bar owners to slow-pour Guinness, just like in the old country. And he not only had taps installed in his bars but arranged to have one put in at the far corner of the screened-in front porch.

On this night, the players around the table were unusually upset because my father was having a piece of Irish luck, with all the cards seeming to fall his way. "You're killing us, Porky," Powers whined. "At least leave enough for the wife and kids."

"Ah, poor Charley," my father commiserated. "You'll just have to go out in your backyard and dig up some of that buried treasure you keep there. You know, the money left over from the last campaign."

"Go on with ya, Porky. There's no such treasure," Powers retorted. "I'm a man of the people, just a poor man of the people."

The groans around the table told me what they all thought of that assertion. Da continued to win, and the men gradually folded, becoming drunken bystanders to the slaughter.

I must've dozed for a while because when I woke up, the

game had come down to Da himself and the diminutive Powers. Porky called and beat two pairs with his own three kings.

"That's it for me," Powers said. "You've cleaned me out." There was a moment's pause. "Actually, Porky . . . ," he stammered, "I need to give you a marker."

Instantly, the atmosphere changed. The coldness that emanated from my father seemed to lower the temperature. Even the drunkest of the men grew silent. "We don't play that game here, Charley," my father said icily. "You know I never accept markers. Like I've always told you, this is a cash-and-carry business."

"But Porky," the man begged, "I just don't have it with me."

"Then write me up a marker for something you do have."

"Like what, Porky?" the man whined. "My house? My car? What?"

"What else have you got, Charlie?" my father asked quietly.

A few nights later, just before dawn, I found out just how the bet had been paid. I always heard my father come in from nights in the pub and wondered which Da I'd get: the happy drunk, full of song and stories of the little people, or the man overcome by the Curse of the Black Irish—when alcohol puts a mood on a man, and the demons come out.

Thankfully, on this night strains of "Wild Colonial Boy" sung horribly off-key by my father and a cohort drifted to me on the breeze as they rounded the corner on Barker Road. But there was another sound, something I couldn't identify, and yet, in some way, I knew I'd heard it before. The men stopped outside the house, and my father came in quietly as if he were sneaking home, forgetting how loud he'd just been singing.

The door to my room crept open, and I heard my Da's stage whisper in the night. "Tommy, are you awake? Wake up, Boyo. I have a surprise for ya."

A surprise? What did he mean?

"Tommy, get up. Come on, boy. This is something you don't want to miss."

I scrambled out of bed and followed my father outside, still in my pajamas. There was a smell in the air I couldn't recognize. What had my father brought?

"Give me your hand, Tommy. That's it. Now, come a little bit forward and touch this."

My fingers felt something warm and smooth, and I pulled my hand back, afraid. "Don't be afraid, boy," my father said. "He's going to be your best friend."

He? What did he mean?

"This is Kentucky Blue, the finest old thoroughbred Suffolk Downs Racetrack ever saw. He's a horse, Boyo. He's Equus. He's a Pegasus. On this magnificent animal, you'll fly like the wind. Now, reach out and get a good feel of him."

I was shaking with excitement as my hands took in the entire animal. Starting at his nose, I ran my fingers over every inch of the huge creature. I couldn't believe the muscle of the shoulder compared to the thin ankle. I loved the flowing mane and the soft ears. And then, the big horse nuzzled me, as if to say, "I'm glad to meet you, little boy, would you like a ride?"

"Think of it, Boyo," my father went on. "How many kids would love to have an animal like this? But only you, Tommy, possess the great Kentucky Blue. There's a word in Gaelic that describes what you'll feel when you ride him. It's *copel*. It means gallop, to run free. Picture it, boy."

My father tapped his chest in the rhythm of a horse galloping as he pronounced, *"Copel, copel, copel . . .* Say it, Tommy. Say it with me. *Copel."*

Now I could see the horse through my father's eyes. *"Copel, copel, copel, copel,"* we chanted.

"Can I ride him, Da? Can I ride him right now?"

It was then we heard the back door slam as my mother and sister arrived. "What in God's name is going on here, Porky, and what is that thing doing in our front yard?"

"Good evening, Marie," my father said amiably. "This magnificent beast, Kentucky Blue by name, will become Tommy's magic carpet. On him, he will shed his disability and take his place in the world of little boys."

"What in God's name are you talking about, Porky?"

My father came close to her, placing a loving arm around her shoulders. "If I know little boys, dear, tomorrow morning the yard will be full of playmates for Tommy, and that's what we really want, now, isn't it?"

My father could always melt my mother's resolve and touch her heart when he spoke to her this way, and that night was no exception.

"You're a *divil* of a man, Porky, a *divil* of a man."

"But you love me, don't you, dearie? Now, give me a big kiss. Come on. Right now. Give me a kiss."

As we moved inside, Porky's friend, Beansy Norton, tied the big thoroughbred to a tree in the front yard. Everyone seemed happy, particularly Kentucky Blue, with a whole lot of grass to nibble and a little boy to love him.

The next morning, my father was up far earlier than usual. In fact, I was just finishing my breakfast when he came downstairs. On this special day there was no hangover, and Da's spirits were bright with enthusiasm.

"Did you finish your breakfast? Ah, that's good, boy, that's good. Let me just have a cup of coffee, and then we'll be going about the business of making you some new friends."

Ten minutes later, we were out on the front lawn with my arm around the neck of the old thoroughbred.

"You know, Tommy, when I was a boy in the old country, we didn't have television, and radio wasn't in everybody's house. So the newspaper boys who worked the streets would spread the front-page news by ringing a large bell and proclaiming what was going on in the world. It got our attention, and that's exactly what you're going to do this fine morning."

"Da?" I queried.

My father held a large bell in his left hand that he rang loudly, shaking it up and down. "You see, boy, you have to cause some excitement. Now, take the bell and ring it, Tommy. Ring it, and announce, 'Come one, come all, Sullivan's pony rides a nickel.'"

I took the bell but hesitated.

"Come on, boy, come on," my father commanded. "Ring the bell and announce to the world that Tommy Sullivan is offering pony rides to every boy and girl in the neighborhood."

In the beginning, my ringing of the bell lacked energy and enthusiasm, but within minutes, kids started to appear. I could hear their voices and sense their excitement.

"Wow, look at that."

"He's beautiful."

"Isn't he something?"

"Gee, he's big."

Now I was ringing the bell with real enthusiasm and calling out, "Sullivan's pony rides a nickel." And as every child arrived, my father would ask their names and introduce them to me. Five, ten, twenty, thirty kids arrived. It was as if a town crier was spreading the good news—Sullivan's pony rides a nickel. The yard filled with girls and boys and noise, all of it music to my ears.

Everyone rode Kentucky Blue, and when we weren't on the horse's back, my father and three of his friends got us into games of leapfrog, "Red Rover," and "Duck, Duck, Goose." It was the most amazing day of my life, until Eddy Mullins and his gang showed up.

I remember my father telling me that four boys had just arrived and were standing at the far end of the yard. "After we finish this ride with Charlie here, Tommy, we'll go and meet them and invite them to participate in this grand event."

By this time, I already felt like an old veteran up on Kentucky Blue's back as we rode around the yard, led by either my father or Beansy. Charlie was afraid, so I got a chance to prove I could be the brave one. "Don't worry, Charlie," I told him. "Kentucky Blue is very gentle. He'll only gallop when we ask him to."

We finished the circuit of the yard, and Charlie jumped down to the ground, helped by my father. It was at that exact moment—when no one was holding the horse—that I heard the *ping* and felt the stone smack into Kentucky Blue's rump. Much later I learned that Eddy Mullins had used a slingshot to send the old thoroughbred flying through the neighborhood.

Like the days when he leaped from a starting gate Blue was off, out of the yard in three long strides. As I struggled to hang on to his neck, I heard my father's yell fading into the distance. "Hang on, Tommy! Hang on!"

My mother was crying, "Oh my God! Oh my God! Get him, Porky! Get him!"

As Kentucky Blue gained speed, I could hear the entire neighborhood chasing us down the street. I should've been afraid, but something wonderful was happening, something amazing. I was experiencing freedom. As the horse picked up speed and I tucked down into his neck, the sound of the wind in my ears, combined with the power of the animal, gave me a feeling I can't describe. It was an experience unlike any I've ever had before or since. I actually began to encourage him. "That's it, Blue. Come on, boy. Run."

But where? Where was the animal going to run? His hooves pounded the cement of the neighborhood streets, and then I felt him rise up and almost lost hold as he soared over something—

a wall or a fence—I didn't know, and I didn't care. I was free, riding on the back of this noble steed, riding like the wind.

And then, it all came to a grinding halt.

I guess Kentucky Blue saw something he just had to stop and eat. Maybe it was a neighbor's flowers or a certain kind of grass. I'm not sure. But the next thing I knew, the animal came to an abrupt stop, and I went flying through the air, over Blue's neck, and landed—thank God—in the middle of someone's soft flowerbed.

I lay there, unsure if I were alive or dead, as the posse of people arrived on the scene. "Oh Jesus, Mary, and Joseph, Tommy," my father said, panting. "Are you alive, boy? Are you all right?"

With the wind knocked out of me, I couldn't answer my Da, but I guess the look on my face said it all. I was wonderful.

8 : WANT TO PLAY?

I T DIDN'T TAKE LONG FOR THE NEWS OF MY RUN-away ride to spread all over town. In fact, by the next morning a newspaper reporter with a cameraman in tow had shown up at our front door in the hopes of writing the story and getting a dramatic picture of a poor little blind boy and his beautiful old horse.

In the meantime, the chief of police, an old gambling pal of Porky's, had been compelled by the woman whose flowers had been eaten by Kentucky Blue to enforce a town ordinance that definitively stated that no horse would be allowed to be ridden, raised, or housed within town limits.

So, when the reporter arrived at our front door, I was surprised by my father's reaction. "I'm so glad you're here," he told him. "I believe you can be very helpful creating public sympathy for my son. I can't believe that any member of the city council would want to take this horse away from a child with a disability."

And so my father, with my mother acting as photo consultant, posed the picture just so. In my left hand, I held an empty bridle. My right arm was draped around the big animal's neck with my head pressed tightly against his flesh. You could almost see the tears falling one at a time down my cheek.

The reporter knew a good story when he heard one, and milked it for all it was worth. When the article appeared the next morning, it was called, "Is Justice Blind?"

"Is justice blind?" it asked. "Or is it our city council that lacks the vision to make an exception in the case of Porky and Marie Sullivan's little blind child, Tommy, and an old thoroughbred named Kentucky Blue? Should a city ordinance, written to encourage the use of automobiles back at the turn of the century, be applied when a little boy's heart is about to be broken? Is the rule of law so inflexible that the special needs of a child cannot be considered? Should Tommy Sullivan never again feel the warmth of an animal that loves him, or have friends flock to his yard to share in the delight of riding such a noble steed? Do we want to be a party to a child's misfortune? Contact your city council members—their names are printed below—and attend next Tuesday's meeting, letting your voices be heard."

I was told that over two hundred people showed up at that meeting, upset by the insensitivity of the city council for maintaining the ordinance. But in the end, Kentucky Blue was placed in a trailer and taken away. What I figure is that some council members had it in for my father. You can't walk the edge of the law as long as Porky did without creating some enemies.

My father always said that the horse went to a wonderful farm upstate in New Hampshire to live out his days. I have to admit, though, it is possible Blue never saw that green grass pasture. I couldn't help but think he might have found his way to "the glue factory." I'll never know. But what I immediately understood was that the world had gone back to the way it had been. I was alone in my yard, and the fence that separated me from life seemed to grow even higher.

For the first time, I knew what it was to be depressed. Within seventy-two hours, I had gone from the high feeling of belonging to the lonely isolation of my backyard, once more disconnected from the kids I so wanted to have as friends. I sat on the swing, listless and lost, with the sounds of the neighborhood school singing a dirge of disappointment in my head. At that moment, I believed I would remain in this bondage of isolation forever, with no hope of freedom.

I'd escaped from Perkins, if only temporarily. I had experienced joy with other children, and had it taken away. The large Braille book that now sat on my lap, unread, reminded me I would be returning to the school for the blind. And then, in that moment of despair, a miracle happened. Not a big miracle, just a couple of four-and-a-half-foot-tall little miracles.

Over the past six months, a house had been built next to ours. I loved the sounds of the men at work and the smell of new wood, freshly cut. There was something hopeful and clean about it. Now it was finished, and a large moving van had pulled into the driveway. More men went to work, moving a family in, and while it was happening, I heard the excited voices of—of what?

Two children, who sounded about my age, were talking on the other side of the fence. *Boys or girls?* I wondered. *Could it be possible that little boys about my age are moving right next door?* My heart fairly leaped—and, just as suddenly, I was sad once more. Why should I get excited? Between them and me was . . . the fence. It was no different from the kids who played in the school playground or on the local baseball field. I was in here, and they were out there.

But wait a minute. There was a difference. And in a moment of clarity, I understood what it was. These little people were playing *in the backyard,* just on the other side of that fence. I could hear one call out to the other, "Come on, Billy, let's play whiffle ball. The yard's perfect for it. You pitch. I want to hit the first homer out."

Then the other voice. "You can't hit my curve, Mikey. You're just gonna whiff at air."

Two little boys were playing ball in the yard next door, and I knew at my core—at the deepest part of my eleven-year-old soul—that I had to get to them. I had to let them know I existed, that I was here. But how? There was only one thing to do, and the moment had come to do it. If I could escape Perkins and voyage down the Charles River, I should be able to break out of this yard and meet—what were their names?—Billy and Mike.

I got off the swing and walked to the fence closest to where the boys were playing. Reaching up, I grabbed hold of the chain link and began the climb, hand-over-hand, foot-over-foot, escaping the confines of my prison. *Reach up. Grab. Dig your feet in. Climb. Reach up. Grab. Dig your feet in. Climb.* And finally, at the top, open space.

Now, an intelligent person would grab hold of the top of the fence, ease his way over, and sort of shimmy down the other side. But I was Tom Sullivan, and this was my statement of freedom. And like the skydiver who yells "Geronimo" and takes the leap of faith, hoping the parachute will open, I launched from the top of the fence.

Only eight feet to the ground, but it was plenty of time to gain speed enough to break a bone or two. I crashed on the hard dirt of the yard next door. The family hadn't planted grass yet, so the landing was—to say the least—a little rough. I got the wind knocked clean out of me, but I didn't care: I heard the running feet of the two boys as they reached my side.

Billy got there first. "Wow," he said, amazed. "That was a cool fall. Are you all right?" I couldn't answer him, so he went on. "I'm Billy Hannon, and this is my brother, Mike. Are you okay?"

I struggled for breath and finally squeezed out, "Yeah, I think so. I'm Tom Sullivan, and I'm blind."

"Wow," the boys said together.

Two sets of hands pulled me to my feet, two voices asking again if I was all right. I stood up and sort of checked to see if everything was still in the right place. Happily, all of the parts seemed to be in working order.

Looking back over my life, I don't know that any single moment meant as much in the scheme of who I became as this one. And I know that—other than when my wife, Patty, first said, "I love you"—no three words ever meant more to me than those uttered by eleven-year-old Billy Hannon.

He asked, simply, "Want to play?"

Did I hear him right? Do I want to play? Was he kidding? Was this real? Nothing else in the entire eleven years of my existence had ever been this important. I had been waiting, aching, wishing, hoping, needing, pleading, and, most of all, praying for this miracle to occur. And now it had.

"Oh sure," I said matter-of-factly. "Let's play."

9 ⁝ SUMMER SOLSTICE

June 21—summer solstice. It was the longest day of the year, and I never wanted it to end because I had found my first friend. I awakened before sunrise, and heard the "cheerio" of the robin nesting in the big oak tree at the far end of our yard. Her joyous song, filled with the spirit of the day, mirrored the feeling in my little boy's heart.

New adventures were in store for Billy and me. Billy owned a Mattel walkie-talkie transmitter and receiver unit that kept us in total communication, just in case there was a great TV show on after we had reluctantly gone home at the end of the day, or in case a ghost, or some spooky thing, woke us up in the middle of the night.

During the first week of our friendship, we ran a wire the sixty feet from Billy's bedroom to my house. The only problem was that the closest window was in my mother and father's bedroom, and I hadn't considered how they'd feel if we were going to have our first morning conversation at, oh, let's say, 6:00 a.m.

The other thing about the radio transmitters was that I really don't think they worked. I mean, when he pushed the "talk" button, I don't know that I ever really heard Billy's voice coming through the speakers. I actually believe that what we did across the open space from his house to mine was yell.

At that time, most of us spent Friday nights at seven o'clock watching *Lassie* on NBC. The two main characters were boys exactly our age—Jeff and Porky. Interesting, huh? My father carried the same moniker.

Jeff and Porky used to call each other across the open fields of their farms with a recognition signal that I still don't quite understand. They'd yell, "Eee-yaw-kee!" and the other would answer, "Eee-yaw-kee!" I don't know if it was an Indian word or some other ancient language, but what I do know was that when my father heard it at six o'clock in the morning, he was not a happy Irishman.

"What in the name of God are you boys doing?" he roared on the morning of summer solstice. "Don't you understand that I didn't get home from work until three o'clock this morning, and now you're waking me up with some stupid 'eee-yaw-kee'? What is 'eee-yaw-kee' anyway?"

"Nothing, Da, nothing," I stammered. "I'm sorry."

I pushed the button in and yelled again. "Billy, I'll see you after breakfast, okay?"

"Okay, Tom," he answered. "Over and out."

"Over and out." And I got out of my parents' bedroom as fast as I could.

Then came the hard part of the morning: waiting for my mother to get up to make me breakfast. Earlier that week, I had tried carrying out this task by myself, and dropped a quart of milk on the floor. Back then milk came in glass bottles, and the liquid river spread the glass out all over the kitchen. What an unbelievable mess, and I couldn't even clean it up. This certainly meant that my mother didn't want me making my own breakfast, and I really couldn't blame her. Like I said, it was a mess. To this day I don't have any real kitchen skills.

So, there I'd be, waiting for my mother to come downstairs and feed me, because a guy needed nourishment if he was going to have all kinds of adventures with his friend, Billy Hannon.

Usually, right in the middle of scrambled eggs and bacon with English muffins, orange juice, and a One-A-Day vitamin pill that my mother always made me take, Billy would arrive. "Good morning, Mrs. Sullivan."

"Good morning, Billy. Have you had your breakfast?"

"Yes, ma'am, but I am still kind of hungry."

Nobody could eat as much as Billy. My friend was a bottomless pit. No wonder he went on to be an outstanding high school and college linebacker. The guy could eat.

So, what to do with long days and limitless imagination? We

planned our strategy while Billy put on the feedbag. If it was baseball, would we play whiffle ball or half-ball—a game played with half a rubber ball that didn't go quite as far when you hit it.

If the tide was out, maybe we'd dig for clams or go to the town pier and fish for smelt, flounder, or mackerel, depending on what was running in the harbor.

Then there was the dark forest up behind the town dump in the old quarry. Mr. Hannon told us that Indians still lurked behind trees and occasionally scalped little boys. Now, that was scary.

But what if it was raining? What would two little guys do if it was raining? Well, if we had money, we could go to the Rialto Theater in Scituate Harbor and see a movie, or maybe go bowling.

Billy introduced me to bowling. Not ten-pin like you see on television, where the ball has holes in it for your fingers, but a game called "candlepin bowling" that I think is only played in New England. In this game, the balls are small—a little bigger than a softball—and the pins are shaped like candles. When you knock them down, the deadwood stays on the alley, making it much more difficult to make spares. A top candlepin bowler scores around one hundred. I loved the game.

Billy figured out that if he tied a piece of string to both ends of the ball return, I could trace my hand along the rope, making my approach to the foul line and rolling the ball down the alley. By the end of our first summer, I bowled an eighty-three—not bad for a guy who couldn't see the pins.

But the best part of rainy days was the kind of play we

designed around our imaginations. And here, in this arena of fantasy, I was the leader. Billy began to listen to dramas on the radio: *The Lone Ranger* and *Hopalong Cassidy*, *Cisco Kid* and *Flash Gordon*. We liked the gangster shows, too: *Gangbusters*, *The Shadow*, *Suspense Theater*, and *Johnny Dollar, Private Eye*. I even got Billy listening to some soap operas, and Billy began to love to play make-believe as much as I did. He understood how to play from a blind kid's point of view.

My Da had given me one of the first reel-to-reel Revere tape recorders. We used this old machine to make our own movies, creating sound effects with whatever we could find around the house. If we played "King Arthur and the Round Table," for example, the knights fought with curtain-rod swords and shields made of garbage can lids. We clanged and struck our way through many battle scenes, saving fair maidens, conquering evil knights, and slaying huge dragons.

Other times, we were cowboys in the Wild West, sitting cross-legged on the floor with our shoes off, making horse sounds by pounding the ground, and banging our heels together, pretending the gun shots were ringing out from our old .44s as we chased Butch Cavendish and the Hole-in-the-Wall Gang over the open range.

Then there were our make-believe Big League baseball games, when we'd pound our fists into Billy's catcher's mitt for pitches and, again, hit our shoes together—this time, as if we were both pounding homeruns over the "green monster" in Fenway Park.

We wrote all the dialog for our characters, and actually I

think some of our plots were pretty good. In this way, as I was entering Billy's world, he was coming to truly love and appreciate mine. No friendship could have deepened as quickly as the one between Billy and me, and it lasted nearly fifty years.

Billy's birthday is on June 21—the longest day of the year. In 1959 my friend turned eleven, and his folks decided they'd let him have a slumber party (or as some called it back then, a pajama party). Billy and Michael were new in the neighborhood, but they were extremely outgoing kids, and during the last two months of school, they had made a number of new friends. When those twenty little boys arrived for the party, you can bet that no one ever got into their pajamas, and nobody slept.

Even though I learned later that Billy didn't like him very much, Eddy Mullins and three of his gang members had been invited to the party. Eddy and his guys loved to pick on weaker and smaller boys, and as the traditional party games began, Big Eddy and his friends stayed on the sidelines, giving the impression that "Pin-the-Tail-on-the-Donkey," "Musical Chairs," and "Beanbag Toss" were beneath their dignity.

I was on the sidelines, too, because only Billy knew how to play with me, and everybody else was still incredibly awkward. I can't blame them. None of them had ever met a blind child before. But there's a big difference between awkward and cruel. Eddy Mullins was cruel.

"Okay," Eddy says, patronizing. "If you can't play the games, why don't you just tell us a bedtime story?"

Now I was in my element—fantasy, make-believe, story-telling—this was something I knew how to do. Instinctively, I understood how to control my audience. "Do you guys know that pirates operated right off the Scituate Coast during the early 1800s?"

I heard the chorus, "Nooooo."

"Well, they did. And they plundered American merchant ships carrying goods and treasures all up and down the eastern seaboard. The most famous of these pirates was a French-Canadian named Edward Carpentier. He and his men would rob the ships and bury the treasure in the woods up around the old quarry."

"Uh-uh," the voices said again. "Really?"

"That's what my father says. But Carpentier had a first mate, a guy named Jamie Martin, who figured he could murder the captain and get a bigger share of the loot himself. You guys know about the Henshaw House up on Third Cliff."

"I heard about it," one of the boys put in. "It's supposed to be haunted."

"I think it is," I told him. "In fact, I'm really sure it is. Carpentier and his men lived there and would watch for ships moving in and out of Boston Harbor from the crow's nest they built up on the roof."

"Yeah," Charlie said, "it's still there."

"So what!" Eddy put in. "That doesn't mean it's haunted."

"Well," I went on, pausing for dramatic effect, "this guy, Martin, murdered the captain and threw his body off the crow's nest into the sea. So for the last two hundred years, the Frenchman has been searching and searching for the lost treasure."

"Wow!" Billy said. "Has anybody actually seen the ghost?"

"I've heard," I added slowly, "that anyone who's lived in the house has been murdered. I know that's what happened to Martin, the first mate that killed Carpentier. Supposedly, they found him with his throat slit, and they could tell from the wounds that it was done with the curved blade of a pirate's dagger that Carpentier always carried. Anyway, I've heard that's why no one lives in the house now."

"You're full of crap, Blindey!" Eddy said. "First of all, there's no such thing as ghosts, and second, I know that the reason no one lives in the house is because it's been condemned by the city 'cuz it's so old."

Billy had a daring idea. "Hey guys, why don't we all sneak over there tonight and go inside? The ghosts can't get all of us."

Nobody volunteered.

"Come on, guys," Billy tried again, "we can do it."

"Not me," somebody said.

"I'm not going in there," another voice added. That sentiment seemed to gain the support of all the boys.

"Well, I'm not going in there alone," Billy said.

I don't know why the thought struck me. To this day, I have no idea why, but in that instant, I spoke up. "I'll go in the house, and I'll stay there all night. I'm not afraid of ghosts. I can't see them. And, anyway, I don't think ghosts hurt people—they're just lonely spirits."

"Yeah," Eddy said, "they're lonely, lonely enough to murder a blind kid."

The yell from the other boys seemed to suggest that they all agreed. And so, there we were—twenty little boys in the dark outside the Harrison House. Billy broke a window using the old Louisville Slugger. He took a swing and knocked in the plywood that had long ago replaced the original glass. Boy, baseball bats come in handy for a lot of stuff when you're eleven years old.

"Okay, Blindey," Eddy said. "Go on in. We'll be back to get you in the morning—or what's left of you."

"Here's the window, Tommy," Billy said. "Let me give you ten fingers."

Ten fingers was a boost up to the window, where you put your foot on your friend's hand and sort of hop up in the air. My climb through the open space could not have been elegant. Actually, I crashed and sort of rolled through the window, bruising my knee and cutting my hand. But none the worse for the wear, I was in the spook house.

I heard the boys beating a quick retreat back down the road, all except for Billy, who was still standing at the window. "Listen, Tommy, I'm not gonna go home with the rest of them. I'll stay here, just in case you need me."

"Thanks, Billy, but I have to do this so that the guys don't think I'm a chicken."

"Really? Honest Injun? Tommy, aren't you afraid?"

I shrugged in the dark. "Yeah," I said. "I'm really scared, but

I have to do this, so I'm gonna go further into the house, and you go home with the other guys. I don't want them to think I'm cheating."

"Okay, Tommy," Billy said hesitantly. "But I'll be back first thing in the morning, right when the sun comes up. You'll hear me."

"Eee-yaw-kee?" I laughed.

"You bet. Eee-yaw-kee. Good luck, Tommy." And my friend was gone.

I know that children are afraid of things that go bump in the night—silhouettes and spectres created by light and dark in a quiet room. There are kids who have to sleep with the light on, or who need their mothers to sit with them and tell them stories until they fall off to pleasant dreams. But I was surprised to learn that night that I, too, had my own demons to face in the dark. My ghosts were not visual illusions but even greater manifestations of fear, because they engaged all of my other senses.

As I rose from the floor, I was aware of the wetness of mold and mildew sticking to my pants leg and my hands. *Slime*, I thought. *Am I being slimed?*

The smell was musty and old, filled with decay and what I perceived as death. My imagination ran wild. *Death*, I thought. *People have been murdered in this house, stabbed and thrown from the balustrade.* And now, here I was—a little boy, a little blind boy in a big, scary place. *Am I alone—or are there spirits here?*

A slow, creepy, crawly, creaking sound. *Oh crap, what was*

that? It came from all around me. Then it stopped. *Oh God, there it is again.*

Looking back, I'm sure the old mansion was just settling or shifting on its foundation, but at the time I wanted to run. Run as fast as a blind person could. Run away from this musty old trap. Get out. Escape. But I couldn't, because the guys would think I was a coward.

So I tried to bluff the darkness. "Okay, ghosts!" I yelled, shaking. "You're not scaring me. Not Tommy Sullivan. I'm gonna stay right here all night, even if you murder me."

I was answered by a scuttling sound—what was it? Feet?—moving close to me in the dark. The squeaks that followed made me understand. *Rats.* I was in a house full of rats. I squeezed up against the wall, figuring that at least then everything would have to come at me from in front. I shivered in the slime and the cold. Something whished across my face, and I screamed. And then I heard a different squeak and the whish of what I decided must be bats.

Rats and bats. Rats and bats. I was in a house full of rats and bats and creaks and squeaks. But so far, no ghosts. Okay.

Then I got really weird. I started to sing, "When you walk through a storm, keep your head up high, and don't be afraid of the dark."

Oh brother, I was really losing it.

But the singing helped, and the house echoed so I sounded pretty good. The only problem was, as I got to the big chorus, "Walk on, walk on, with hope in your heart, and you'll never walk alone," the rats started to move down front like they were looking for a better seat. *God.* Something ran over my shoe. I kicked at it and missed.

Hour after hour, I counted sheep—or were they rats?—and sang, reminding myself why I was there, and prayed. Squeaks and creaks, bangs and clangs. The night moved on inexorably slow. Seconds. Minutes. Hours. When would the daylight come?

I must have dozed standing up, leaning on the wall, because I was jolted awake by the sound of Billy's call.

"Eee-yaw-kee!" I heard.

"Eee-yaw-kee!" I croaked. "Eee-yaw-kee."

In an instant, Billy was through the window, hugging me. "Are you all right, Tommy? Were there any ghosts?"

"Naw," I said, full of boyish bravado. "Piece of cake."

And it was all worth it as he helped me through the window, and I heard the cheers of the boys.

10 ⦂ FOG BOUND

Billy's dad, John Hannon, liked to fish. Actually, that's not quite true. John Hannon loved to fish. He was obsessed with spending his summers on the ocean in pursuit of anything that would bite fresh bait. In the waters off New England, he preferred to fish for blues, bass, and an occasional tuna. However, he'd settle for all of the bottom stuff—cod, haddock, flounder. He'd even take the small ones you'd get when you trolled along the coastline—mackerel and pollack. Those weren't any good to eat, but they still were a lot of fun to catch.

Billy had developed the same passion as his father for the sport, and we spent a lot of our afternoons sitting on the town

pier in Scituate Harbor with drop lines, hoping to catch anything—even a perch or a skate. And you know what? I came to
love all of it, too. I suppose just being with Billy was my princi-
pal motivation, but the fishing certainly added to the fun. Mr.
Hannon owned a twenty-one-foot Novie with a small, protected
cabin. These boats were called Novies because they were built in
Nova Scotia, principally out of oak and maple, with an overlap
design that allowed for double strength nailing and caulking.
They were, pound-for-pound, the most seaworthy craft available
to New England fishermen at that time.

He powered it with a big Johnson outboard that sounded like
an old jalopy when you got up to speed. But it did the job. Mr.
Hannon kept the boat as neat as a pin, and he must've spent as
much time cramming it just so with fishing gear as he did out on
the water. Everything had its place, and he was finicky to the nth
degree regarding the ship-shape nature of his craft. She was
called Bonnie Mary after Billy's mother, Mary Hannon, and I
loved it when the call would come—sometimes by phone, and
sometimes on the walkie-talkie—telling me to be ready at five
o'clock the next morning to "go out after the big ones."

We'd fish the coastline from Cohasset to Marshfield and
back. John Hannon knew every inlet and rock outcropping
where bass or blues might be hiding. This was before the Coast
Guard had forced anglers to carry radios and way before the
development of the Global Positioning System (GPS). So, when
you fished the New England coast, you were virtually out there
on your own.

I don't know why it is that the simplest food always tastes so good when you eat it out on the water. Mrs. Hannon would prepare tuna sandwiches on white bread and ham and cheese loaded with heavy mustard on what we called "booky" rolls, bought at the local delicatessen in Scituate Harbor. These rolls were hard as a rock, but for some reason they tasted great with ham and cheese and a lot of mustard.

Mr. Hannon would let me bring my transistor radio, and on many days, we'd fish while listening to afternoon Red Sox baseball games. *Man*, I thought, *life could never get any better than this.* We were fishing off the mouth of the North River on a pristine summer day when the ocean was glassy and flat. I had my shirt off, and the sun warmed my shoulders as we trolled slowly in pursuit of bluefish.

Of all the fish inhabiting the waters around Scituate, blues were the best at fighting and the most fun to catch. They ran from two to ten pounds, and they were fierce in their desire to maintain their freedom. Sometimes, you fished them with live sea worms or clams, but if you were trolling, you used a lure. When they hit, if you were fishing with light tackle and a six-pound test line, you were in for the thrill of your life.

Mr. Hannon had heard on the fishing report the night before that schools of blues had been sighted, and so our anticipation was heightened. We had already worked our way from Scituate Harbor down the coast to Marshfield. And now, in the early afternoon, we had turned and were coming back. No luck yet, but were we disillusioned or upset? Absolutely not. The possibility that we would hit a school of blues was always just around the corner of the next shoal. I was thinking just that when I heard it.

"Mr. Hannon! Mr. Hannon!" I cried. "Stop the boat—they're out there!"

"What are you talking about, Tommy?" John said, as he threw the Bonnie Mary into neutral.

"Cut the motor, Mr. Hannon, and listen!"

I had heard the smack of fish jumping and knew it *had* to be blues. As it got quiet, Billy and Mr. Hannon heard it, too.

Smack—Smack—Smack-Smack!

"Okay, boys," Mr. Hannon announced, "I just saw them. We're in a school. A big one. It's gonna be fun now. You two fish, and I'll help you bring 'em in. There's gonna be some big-time action. Boy, oh boy, oh boy!"

And it happened just then.

ZING!

My line flew off the reel as a bluefish struck.

"Keep your tip up, Tommy. Keep that rod tip up in the air!" Mr. Hannon yelled. "Watch your drag, watch your drag! You don't want to lose him."

I whooped as the blue jumped, smacking down on the water doing everything in its power to escape.

ZING!

Now Billy had one on his line. What a day!

"Be careful, boys, be careful," Mr. Hannon called again. "Don't get the lines crossed."

When you fight a blue, you have to move with the fish around the boat rail, or he'll snap your line and be gone. Mr. Hannon had taught me how to keep my line from tangling with other fishermen, so Billy and I worked together over the next two hours to land a number of crafty bluefish. My arms and shoulders ached with the effort, but I was as happy as a little eleven-year-old boy could be.

We caught twenty-six blues that day. Billy landed fifteen, and I brought in eleven. Toward the end, I gave my pole to Mr. Hannon, and he added five more blues to our catch, bringing the total to thirty-one. Thirty-one bluefish. In all the days I fished the waters off Scituate, I never again came close to catching that many. The sweat was pouring down my back, and I noticed that I had started to shiver. I reached into my backpack and pulled on a windbreaker.

"It's getting cold, Mr. Hannon," I said.

"That's not all boys," he told us. "We're in for a problem. I should have been paying more attention to the sky. Fog's rolled in, and it's gonna be pea soup out here."

"Pea soup?" I asked. "What do you mean?"

"Tommy," John Hannon laughed, "in about ten minutes, I'm gonna be as blind as you. We may be out here a lot longer than expected."

Even an old salt like Mr. Hannon couldn't predict New England weather. In fifteen minutes, the glassy water had turned to chop and then to waves that threw the little Novie around like a matchbox.

"Hang on, boys," John said. "Hang on! We're going to have to power up and aim directly into the waves. We can't just sit here and take a pounding, or we'll capsize."

There was real anxiety in Billy's dad's voice. We were in danger, and something had to be done.

Everything had become slippery. The sky had opened up as it only can in a New England squall, the rain pelted down in sheets. Mr. Hannon had us moving away from the rocks, keeping his bow into the waves, but the squall was capricious and the wind was swirling, making it impossible for us to set a definite course. We were literally blind as we tried to find a pattern in the waves.

"Tighten those life preservers, boys," Mr. Hannon told us. "Tighten them down good!"

We all understood that this was not fun anymore. Our very lives were at stake, we realized, as a wave crashed over the open boat, soaking us to the bone.

"Oh God!" Billy cried. "Oh God!"

That was just what I was praying. *God, help us.* And then I heard it far off in the distance—the sound of the old bell buoy that marked the entrance to Scituate Harbor—and beyond it the faint calling of the foghorn at the top of Minot Lighthouse.

"Mr. Hannon, Mr. Hannon, I hear the bell buoy and the foghorn. Turn right. I mean, to starboard! I'll try to guide us in."

I climbed forward onto the bough of the boat, slipping as I moved, my hands grasping for a firm hold as the waves buffeted us back and forth, all the while my focus locked onto the sound.

"Just a little to port, Mr. Hannon. That's it. Now straighten it out!"

As I listened, the foghorn was a better line because the bell buoy was being tossed from side to side in the waves, changing the angle of the sound. Moving through the darkness, I sometimes would lose a fix on where we were going and struggled again and again to rediscover the audio beam that would bring us home to safety. After about twenty minutes, I sensed we were rounding the point at Minot Lighthouse because the winds seemed to be dropping.

"That-a-boy, Tommy!" Mr. Hannon said. "We're almost to the mouth of the harbor. I can see the beacon now. Come on down from the bough. I think I can take her in!"

Billy hugged me as I dropped, exhausted, onto the deck. "Wow, Tommy, you saved our lives. You're the bravest guy I know."

"I don't think so, Billy," I told him. "I think I'm just the luckiest."

Whatever. We were all extremely happy to place our feet down on dry land. Billy and Mr. Hannon told my parents that I was a hero, but I knew that I had been as frightened as they were. All that had happened was I had come to understand the power of my own senses, and that being blind didn't have to be a handicap.

On that day, I began to believe that I could turn every disadvantage of my disability into the glorious advantages of my ability. For the first time, I believed in myself, and it felt good. Real good.

11 ⦂ THE QUARRY

YEP, RIGHT ABOUT THEN I WAS AN ELEVEN-YEAR-old on top of the world. "God is in his heaven, all is right with the world." I was a hero, and I had a best friend. How much more could any kid want?

So why is it that when everything seems perfect, fate steps in, shuffles the deck, and comes up with a joker?

It was right after the July 4th weekend, and my father had helped me establish even more independence by buying me a bicycle built for two. That's right, a Schwinn tandem that gave Billy and me a set of wheels that, powered by two sets of legs, could transport us rapidly to every adventure in the neighborhood.

My mother was completely against the bike. She was sure
I'd get hurt, but Dad just went ahead with it anyway. I heard
them arguing about it at night. It was the first of many arguments over me and my freedom. But at the time, I couldn't see
past the beautiful bike that I polished so vigorously, I probably
wore the paint off it.

In 1959, one of the coolest things to do if you were an eleven-
year-old boy with a new bike was to put a balloon or baseball
cards through the spokes of the wheels to create a sound when
the bike moved. We thought it was like the roar of a Harley-
Davidson motorcycle. I liked using a balloon best because the
rubbing of rubber created just the right audio effect. And with
the tandem going maybe twenty-five miles an hour down a steep
hill, we thought we were really big-time guys.

We had just rounded the point of Minot Lighthouse on the
way home from fishing when I heard not just one but a whole
convoy of bikes with stuff in their spokes roaring up behind us.
Billy looked over his shoulder. "Tom, it's Eddy Mullins and the
gang. Let's let them catch us and then kick their butts going
down this hill."

What a concept, I thought. We could show them just how fast
we were.

The convoy surrounded us, and the sound was incredible.
Over the din, I heard Eddy Mullins yell, "There's Blindey. How
are ya, Blindey?"

I tightened my grip on the handlebars and waited for Billy's
signal. "Okay, Tom," Billy said. "Let's bury 'em."

Our two sets of legs galvanized as one, and we lifted the tandem to unbelievable speed as if we were riding on the wind. I whooped with delight as the air buffeted my face and the sound of the other bikes receded. We were invincible—unbelievable—unbeatable. We ruled.

The tires squealed as Billy rounded the corner at the bottom of the hill. He was going too fast, but he maintained control and we rocketed down my street and spun into the driveway. Billy completed the victory by doing a wheelie that almost knocked me off the backseat. What a moment! What a feeling!

The other bikes pulled up behind us, and I could hear the grudging admiration of some of the gang members as they congratulated Billy on the ride.

Before I had a chance to gain some of the accolades, Eddy Mullins, smarting from the embarrassment of being beaten, halted the conversation. "Shut up," he told the gang. "They had four legs, and we were going downhill. Anybody with four legs can beat anybody with two. What's the big deal?"

I don't know why, but I couldn't help but say it. "The big deal, Eddy Mullins, was that we kicked your butt. Yeah. We kicked your butt!"

Eddy got right in my face. "I'll kick your butt right now, Blindey. Come on, I'll kick your butt right now!"

Uh-oh. In an instant I knew that I had made a mistake. I thought, *I don't know how to fight. I'm going to get killed.*

Thank God, Billy jumped in. "Cut it out, Eddy," Billy said.

"You're just a sore loser. Leave Tommy alone, or you'll have to fight both of us."

Billy wasn't as big as Eddy, but the bully could tell he meant it, so he changed his tune. "Okay, Hannon, okay. Why are you hanging out with Blindey here anyway? You could be a member of the gang if you wanted to."

"I'm happy right here," Billy said with conviction, "hanging with Tommy."

"Hey, Eddy," Billy suggested, "why don't you make us both members of the gang?"

"Forget it," Eddy said. "There's no way we're taking *him*."

"I don't want to be in your stupid gang," I told him, not really meaning it. "I don't want to be in your stupid gang at all."

"Well, good luck, Hannon," Eddy continued. "You're gonna really miss a cool day. Me and the fellas are on our way to the quarry."

It was as if a chill came into the air. *The quarry*. I had heard about it all summer from Billy. The old quarry was where gang members went to pass their initiation by jumping off rocks into the murky water below.

"We got three new guys in the gang," Eddy said. "It's their initiation day. I'll bet you haven't got the guts to jump, Hannon."

"Shut up," Billy said.

"No guts, Hannon, no guts."

"I got the guts, Eddy," Billy retorted, the pride and anger ringing in his tone. "I got more guts than you."

"Then come with us and prove it. Show us that you can be a

member of the Warriors. Come on." Eddy turned and grabbed his bike as the signal for the others to follow.

I could hear the concern in Billy's voice. "I gotta go, Tommy. I gotta do this. Listen, I'll come right back as soon as I've jumped, but I gotta do this."

I didn't answer my friend. I felt betrayed. More than that, I felt lost and alone. When it all came down to it, there were still two worlds—mine and theirs—and they were telling me I didn't belong. Even in my hurt and disappointment, I could still hear the concern in Billy's voice. "Really, Tommy, I'll be right back. You know where you are, right? You're at the base of the apple tree in your front yard."

"I can take care of myself, traitor." The words were out before I had a chance to think. To this day, I'm so sorry I said that and hurt my friend, Billy Hannon.

He just got on his bike and said, "I'll be back, Tommy."

I heard the sound of the tires as all the guys headed off down the street. I knew that they would ride their bikes just a couple of blocks and leave them at the edge of the woods that led up to the town quarry. I'd been there a few times with my father, just for walks, and so I kind of knew the lay of the land. As the sound of the bikes receded, I made a decision. *They may not want me to go to the quarry. They may not want me in their gang. They might not want me in their world, but I am not going to stay on the outside anymore. I am going to beat my way in.*

I ran in the house, and without even speaking to my mother in the kitchen, I grabbed my cane and made my way out to the street. As quickly as I could, I tapped my way along, listening for the sound of the boys. By the time I had reached the end of the block, they had left their bikes and were moving through the woods. I could hear them in the distance. *Just follow the sound*, I thought. *Just follow the sound.*

Ow! A tree branch whipped across my face, and I felt the blood ooze from a cut somewhere around my eye. *Slow down, Tommy, slow down. You can't move that fast.* I tripped on a tree root and went down hard, cutting my right knee. Now the sound was lost. I couldn't hear the boys. *Where am I? Stand still and think, Tommy. Just stand still and think.*

Oh, there they are again. I can hear them up ahead and a little to the left. SPLASH—SPLASH! "Yeah!" I heard the cry and knew that the boys had begun to jump off rocks. The rocks all had names: Heart Attack, Death Drop, Niagara Falls—and the big one, Suicide. Billy had told me that he had never heard of anyone who'd jumped off Suicide Rock and lived. It was at the top of the cliff, some sixty feet above the water, with all kinds of outcroppings you could hit on the way down. Billy said that over the years, fifteen people had died attempting the jump.

Oh God. I fell again, and this time I twisted my ankle. The pain was unbelievable, but somehow I pulled myself back up onto my feet. I just had to keep going. Now I was without my cane. I had lost it in one of the falls. So I groped my way toward the sound, parting the bushes with my hands.

I could tell I was close, and I began to understand how far

below me the boys were. Obviously, they had climbed down the side of the quarry and were jumping from ten, fifteen, or twenty feet above the water. I was walking on loose pebbles that slid under my feet, and as I got close to the water, I heard some of them drop away over the edge. In my head, I calculated the time—one thousand one, one thousand two, one thousand three. It seemed that the pebbles fell for three seconds. What did that mean? Ninety feet? Naw, Billy had said sixty, but I counted one thousand-one, one thousand-two, one thousand-three. I zoned in on the boys, working my way forward until I was just above the splashing.

At that moment, Billy looked up. "Oh my God, Tommy. Oh my God, get back! You're too close to the edge. You'll fall. Get back, Tommy!"

In that second, everything seemed to stop. Nobody moved. In the depth of the quarry, there wasn't a sound until Eddy broke the silence. "Hey, Blindey, what are you doing?"

I didn't answer him, so he went on. "Don't you think you'd better go back to Mummy? I'm sure she's worried about you."

"Shut up, Eddy," I heard my voice echo in the space below.

"Well, if you're not going back to Mummy, what are you going to do? Jump? From up there? That's Suicide Rock, Blindey. People have died from up there. You don't want to die, do ya, Blindey?"

"Shut up, Eddy," Billy cried. "Just shut up! Tommy, I'm coming up to get you. Stay right there. I'm climbing up to get you."

"No, Billy. Stay right where you are. I have to do this."

"What are you talking about, Tommy? You don't have to do anything. Don't move until I get up there."

I eased my way closer to the edge, hearing more pebbles drop into the abyss. Now even Eddy was concerned. "Hey Blindey! Just stay right there until Hannon climbs up. Stay right there!"

Forty-five years have passed since that day in July, forty-five wonderful years. My life has been full of love and adventure, struggle and triumph. So why would I risk everything, jumping from Suicide Rock? Because I had to force myself into the world. I had to make a place. It wasn't enough to just share my friendship with Billy. I wanted much more—so much more. And so . . .

"Geronimo," I cried, leaping into space.

The drop to the water below took only seconds, but the impact on my life when I hit the water and survived still plays out every day. I landed hard, knowing immediately that I had hit a rock just under the surface. The pain in my back nearly knocked me unconscious, but the cold water kept me alert. I couldn't breathe and my legs wouldn't work, so I was drowning until hands pulled me to the surface. I guess I was in shock, because all I understood was that I was alive.

Had the risk been worth it? Only time would decide, but the leap from Suicide Rock sent me on a course of risk taking that has allowed me to become a successful adult with a place in the world. Somehow, Billy and the boys got in touch with the police, and I was rushed to South Shore Hospital emergency room.

My parents arrived as the doctor was cleaning up my cuts.

"Your son's a lucky boy, Mr. and Mrs. Sullivan—a very lucky boy. You could have lost him up there. I've been at this hospital for five years and was on-call when two other kids were brought in who were not so lucky. They gotta close that quarry. They just have to close that awful quarry!"

My mother's voice was shaking. "Tommy, what in God's name were you doing at the quarry, and how did you even get there?"

"I followed the guys," I said sheepishly. "I just listened to the sound and followed the guys."

"But why did you jump? Why did you jump from that rock?"

At that moment, I couldn't answer my mother. I guess I didn't really understand the truth myself.

Thank goodness my father answered for me. "He jumped, Marie, because his desire to be part of the world is more important to him even than living, and we have to begin to pay attention."

I heard my parents move to either side of the emergency room table as if squaring off to fight, and I was in the middle.

"Oh, we're gonna pay attention, Porky!" my mother said. "From now on, he's going to be working a lot harder to get ready to go back to Perkins—to a place where he can be safe and learn."

"You mean a place where he can be isolated and alone, Marie!"

"No, I mean a place where blind people *belong*!"

"Our son, Marie, *belongs*. Our son," my father repeated,

"belongs wherever he wants to be. And what he's telling us is that he wants to be part of life, like any other kid his age."

"He'll take his place in the world, Porky, when he's better prepared. And that preparation will come by being smarter than the other people—and more talented. That's how Tommy will find a place to *belong*."

"Not by nearly killing himself, chasing around other boys in the woods," the doctor put in. "You can take him home, Mr. and Mrs. Sullivan. I don't think there are any internal injuries, but keep in touch with us. If he vomits or seems drowsy—anything at all that might be out of the ordinary—come back."

My parents drove me home in silence and sent me to my room. My mother said that I was grounded and could not play with Billy or anyone else for the rest of the summer. I was back in the yard behind the fence, and the world I so desperately wanted to become a part of was now even further away.

12 ⦂ FAITH AND FRIENDSHIP

I WAS OVERWHELMED BY THE LONELINESS. SITTING on the tree swing at the far end of my yard on a perfect summer day, I simply was overwhelmed. For a few brief, shining moments, I had been in the real world—a bird on the wing—no, an eagle taking flight. I had experienced freedom, and now the clang of my gate was as ominous as if it were a cell door placing me in solitary confinement with no hope of escape.

My mother, the guard, had forbidden me to play with Billy, and though they had argued about it my father had given in, agreeing that I would return to Perkins in the fall. From one prison to another—that's how I saw my fate. And for the first time in my young life, the sounds of the world drifting to me on the summer breeze meant absolutely nothing. I vaguely heard a door slam and Billy's voice telling his mother that he was on the way to the ball game.

As he passed by my fence, he stopped. "Hi, Tommy. Wanna see my uniform?"

I didn't move from the swing.

He went on, trying to get my attention. "I'm on the Orioles, and the colors are really cool. Do you wanna see?"

I remained still.

"Aw, come on, Tommy, check it out."

Reluctantly, I got off the swing and crossed to the fence. Like a prisoner through the bars, I stuck my fingers through the chain link and felt his shirt with his name and numbers on the back.

"Aw, come on, Tommy," he pleaded, "talk to me."

I didn't answer.

"Look, I know it's my fault. I should've stopped you from jumping into the quarry."

I heard the sadness in my friend's voice and softened. "Forget it, Billy. It was all my fault. I'm the guy who jumped. It was all my fault."

"Listen," he said. "Why don't we just break you out of here, and you can come to the game with me? It can't get any worse. Your folks are already saying I can't play with you, so let's escape."

"I want to. Boy, do I want to, Billy, but my mother says I have to go back to Perkins today and show the director that I've changed and that when I come back there next fall I'll be a good boy."

The kitchen window banged open. "Billy Hannon!" my mother yelled. "You're not supposed to be talking to Tommy. He's going back to the blind school."

"I'm sorry, Mrs. Sullivan," Billy stammered. "See ya later, Tommy."

"See ya, Billy."

My last hope for freedom walked away down the driveway, headed for the baseball field and out of my life. Or so I believed.

An hour later I was scrubbed, cleaned up, and in stiff, new clothes that I hated. I sat, head down, beside my mother as she drove us up the Southeast Expressway, headed for Perkins.

We were silent—me because I was so depressed and angry, and my mother because I suppose she didn't know what to say. She was committed to this course of action, but I'm sure she hated the feeling between us as much as I did.

I loved my mother. Our relationship had always been as special as mine was with my father. She was the person who taught me music. She read aloud to me at night, prompting me to appreciate good books for as long as I can remember. She was the one who told me what things looked like and understood how much I knew about the world through my other senses. And yet, here we were, driving to Perkins, with my mother committed to her decision about what she thought was right, and me just as committed to being a part of the world outside my backyard and away from the Perkins School for the Blind.

The chimes in the old bell tower struck three as we pulled into the circular drive in front of the administration building. Finally, the silence was more than my mother could take. Turning to me, she said, "Tommy, I don't like this any more than you do, but you're coming back here because I love you, and I know it's the best thing for you."

I remained impassive and silent.

My mother took a deep breath, trying to collect herself. "Tommy, when you were born," she began, "you were the most beautiful baby anyone had ever seen. But you got here too early. I've told you that, right?"

I nodded.

"It was touch-and-go there for a while. You were three pounds four ounces when you were born, and you lost nearly a pound in the first three weeks. I begged God to let you live, and when we brought you home, I knew it was a miracle and that God had answered my prayers. About three months later, I realized that something must be wrong with your eyes. You never looked at a light, and even though you followed people's voices by turning your head, I noticed that you were never in focus. I don't think anybody else figured this out, but mothers—well, we have special instincts about our children, we always seem to know just what's wrong. So I made an appointment at Mass General Hospital with a famous doctor named Frederick Verhoeff. At the time, Verhoeff was considered the best ophthalmologist in the world."

Now I was getting interested. "Ophthalmologist?" I asked.

"An eye doctor, Tommy. He looked at your eyes, and after a lengthy examination turned to your father and me and said, 'Mr. and Mrs. Sullivan, your son is blind. I suggest you institutionalize him.'"

"What does that mean, Mum?" I asked. "Institutionalize?"

"Well, to the doctor, Tommy, it meant to isolate you, put you away somewhere."

"Isn't that what you're trying to do?" I burst out. "Isolate me? Keep me in the backyard? Keep me in a school for the blind?"

"No, Tommy!" my mother answered sharply. "I want you to become educated and artistic. I want you to keep growing in your love for music and books. I want you to be so smart that the world has to give you a place. Do you understand, Tommy? I want the world to make room for you, and for that to happen, you have to be special."

"But I don't have to be different," I said. "I don't have to be alone. Da says I need to be in the world with other kids."

"I want you in the world, Tommy, but you can't be there if you're not special. To everyone, you're handicapped, and the only way you can succeed is to overcome your disability with a talent."

"Let me go to public school, Mum. Let me play with other kids—be part of their world. That's what I want."

"Someday, Tommy, someday," my mother said, shaking her head. "Right now, you're going to go to Perkins, and that's the way it is. Come on, it's time for us to visit Dr. Waterhouse."

On impulse, my mother reached over and hugged me. "I

love you, Tommy. I love you more than anything. I know you're angry with me, and I know you don't understand, but I'd give up my life for you. You're the most important thing in my life, and I know I'm doing the right thing. Please trust me, Tommy."

I could hear the tears in my mother's voice and gave in. "Okay, Mum," I said. "It's okay. Please don't cry. I'll go back to Perkins."

We were both crying, blowing our noses and wiping our eyes.

My mother tried to laugh. "Listen," she said, "I know that Dr. Waterhouse is a little stiff, but let's go in there and give him some Irish charm."

We climbed out of the car and walked together to the administration building. The meeting with Director Waterhouse went rather well. My mother persuaded him that I had been keeping up on all of my schoolwork and that I would return to Perkins that fall a changed boy.

For my part, I tried to smile and assure the director that I wouldn't be any more trouble. After about twenty minutes, Dr. Waterhouse suggested that I go out onto the playground and see some of the boys who were there for summer school while he continued to talk to my mother.

"You'll be pleased to know, Thomas," he said, "that your cohorts in crime, Gerard and Ernest, are part of the summer programming. Their parents felt they needed a little bit of old-fashioned discipline to quiet their desire for escape. You can go outside now. I'm sure they'll be delighted to see you."

As I walked out through the courtyard, I was struck by the

beauty of the place. Perkins wasn't really a prison. All of my senses were alive with the smell of flowers and freshly cut grass, the sound of a myriad birds and the ripple of the stream that kept fresh water always pumping into the pond where we had stolen the rowboat for our Charles River adventure.

A game of modified soccer was going on at the far end of the athletic field. Soccer for the blind is modified by allowing players to touch the ball with their hands, and by using a ball about five times the size of a real soccer ball. The game is no less intense than in a conventional game; the players kick it back and forth, listening for the sound of the bell inside the leather.

I waited until the ball came in my direction and then chased it down and made a rush for the goal. "Hey, who's got the ball?" somebody yelled. "There's somebody else in the game."

Ernie was the goalkeeper, and I blasted a kick at the sound of the buzzer marking the net and heard it stop the buzz, signaling a goal.

"See?" I yelled. "You blindies need me on this team!"

The response from all of my friends was terrific. "Tommy!" some of them yelled. "Hey, Sully, glad you're here!" some others put in. "Boy, we missed you, pal."

I found Ernie and hugged him. Jerry waddled up, and I hugged him, too. I was surprised to realize that I really missed these guys. We had shared a lot of good times together, and especially our escape. I knew right then that these boys would be my friends forever.

We all sat down under a tree, and for the next half hour the guys quizzed me about my summer adventures. They *oohed* and *ahhed* when I told them about fishing, the tandem bike, Billy Hannon, and my leap into the quarry. Eventually, I asked them about how they were handling summer school.

Jerry groaned. "Oh, same ol', same ol'," he said.

Ernie's next question surprised me. "So, why are you back here, Tommy?"

"What do you mean?" I said.

"I mean, why are you here today?" he pressed.

I shrugged. "Because my mother is making me come back."

There was a collective "No!" from the guys—all the guys. I was taken back.

Ernie spoke for them all. "You can't come back here, Tommy. We don't want you here."

"What do you mean?" I stammered. "Aren't we friends?"

"Sure, we're friends, Tommy," Jerry said. "But if you come back here, we've failed."

"What are you talking about?" I asked. "Failed?"

"Tommy," Ernie went on, "don't you remember what we always said—that we were in here, and there was a world out there? Well, you're in that world now, and Jerry's right—if you fail, we all fail."

I was quiet on the ride home. The words of my friends kept rattling around in my head—*if you fail, we all fail.* I understood for the first time that finding my place in the real world was even more important than I had ever believed.

That night, lying in my bed unable to sleep, the words of my blind friends still echoed in my head—*if you fail, we all fail.*

13 ⦂ PITCH AND CATCH

ONCE AGAIN I WAS BACK IN THE YARD, THE world seeming to be further away than ever before. Loneliness had been replaced by utter and total sadness, and the weight of it had taken all of the fight out of me. I sat sullen on my swing, reading my assignments with nothing actually registering in my brain. I was broken—a shattered kid without the competitive anger that had sparked my escape from Perkins and my leap from the quarry.

My father and mother were arguing again, and as was often the case during that summer, the argument was about me. I wondered if they ever thought about the fact that I could hear them as they talked about me. It made me feel like an object tossed back and forth, like a baseball with a pitcher and a catcher.

My father was speaking. "Look at him out there, Marie, with nothing to do and no one to play with. He might as well be a vegetable."

"It's just temporary," my mother said. "He's agreed to go back to Perkins, and when he does, everything will be all right."

"Marie, I'm telling you. In fact, I'll bet you a hundred that within two months he breaks out of there again."

That made me feel kind of good, except that right now I didn't want to escape from anywhere.

"We've been over this and over this, Porky, and you just don't seem to get it. Tommy needs Perkins. He needs the specialized attention they give to every blind child, and I'm going to make sure he gets it."

I heard my father sigh. "Some day, my stubborn wife, you're going to figure out that Tommy is many things, and only one of them is that he's sightless. Maybe if we forgot about it, it wouldn't be such a big deal."

"It's the biggest deal, Porky," my mother said, angrily. "I made a bargain with God that if he let Tommy live, I'd make sure my little boy would grow up to be special, and that's exactly what I'm going to do."

The argument ended abruptly, and I heard the front door slam. Seconds later, I heard my father driving off in the big Oldsmobile. I wasn't sure where he was going, but I figured he wouldn't be home for quite a while—maybe even a couple of days.

When Da left like that, my mother always said he was working, but my sister, Peg, and I understood early on that our father
was an alcoholic and that when he left home angry, it probably
meant he was going on a bender. We'd see him after a couple of
days when he'd come home to sober up.

The hardest part of my childhood had always been trying to
figure out which dad would be returning on a given day—the
happy one who was on the upside of his drinking—or the dangerous, angry, depressed one who was coming down the other
side of the alcohol high. I never knew, and that tension played
out all through my childhood. My father sustained himself with
the bottle while my mother was sustained by faith.

I have always believed in the power of prayer. I asked for a
little boy to come into my life, and Billy Hannon appeared.
True, I had also asked not to be blind, and God hadn't performed that miracle yet. My mother always said that God
probably had His reasons, and because of her fervent belief I
went along with the way she thought.

Anyway, I was still sitting on the swing an hour later when
the big Oldsmobile rolled back into the driveway. A short time
later, Da opened the gate and crossed to the swing. "Still sittin'
here, Boyo? Feeling sorry for yerself, I suppose. Well, that's
good. That'll get ya somewhere in life."

Da's tone was sarcastic. "What's the date today?" he asked.

"July 18," I said.

"July 18. July 18. Well, that means you have about forty days
to sit right here on this swing and become a vegetable before
your mother puts you back in the institution."

My radio was on in the far corner of the yard. The Red Sox were playing the Baltimore Orioles. Da abruptly changed the subject. "What's happening with the Sox, Tommy?"

"Last of the fifth," I told him. "They lead four to one. Tom Brewer is pitching great. He just gave up a homerun to Brooks Robinson, but I think he's still in good control of the game."

"Well, we'll keep the radio on, but I want to show you something. Stand up."

My father placed an object in my hand. "What do you think that is, Tommy?"

I knew right away. "It's a baseball," I said.

"Oh no, it's not. It's an official, major league Spalding. I got it last night at the bar from one of the equipment managers of the Sox. He owed me money on some bets, so I took a trade, and this ball is just part of what I got. Let me show you something else."

My father placed a big league catcher's mitt in my hands. I could smell the leather.

"Wow!" I said. "This is really cool, Da."

"All broken in, too," my father said. "Sammy White used it last week against the Washington Senators."

My dad took it back and put it on his hand, banging the ball into the pocket. "Oh, that feels good, Tommy. When that ball smacks into the old mitt, you can hear the umpire call, 'Strike three.' I've got some other things to show you, Tommy, but you'll have to hug me to see 'em."

Automatically I hugged my Da and laughed. He was wearing

a Big League chest protector, just like the real catchers. A second later, he had a mask on. His voice became muffled as he pulled the straps in place. Now I was completely into what my father was doing. But what did he have in mind?

"Listen, Tommy," he went on, "a catcher's no good with all this gear on, unless he's got a pitcher to throw him strikes."

I thought he meant Billy at first. "Mom said I couldn't play with Billy anymore, Da, and he's down the street in his own game."

"That's right," my father said. "So I guess we'll have to find someone else, won't we? How about a blond right-hander who can really bring some heat? What do you think, Boyo?"

It started to dawn on me. My father wanted *me* to pitch.

"Come here," he said, walking me to the far end of the yard. "Now, stand still. I'll be right back."

Minutes later my father emerged from the garage with a board, some old carpet, and a hammer and nails. Over the next twenty minutes, he built me a pitcher's mound. "Now let's see," he said, his enthusiasm contagious. "The Big League pitcher's mounds are sixty feet six inches from home plate. I talked to the commissioner of the Little League this morning, and he told me that the kids pitch from forty-six feet, so let's measure that.

Da produced a tape measure from his pocket. "Hold this," he said, "right there on the middle of the mound. Now, I'll walk it off. One, two, three, four . . ."

About fifteen steps later, my father stopped exactly forty-six feet away. "So, now we need—let's see—a home plate."

Again, he fashioned one from a piece of old wood, and we

were ready. "All right, Tommy," he said, coming back to me. "First, we're going to work on motion. I think instead of making you an over-the-top, right-handed thrower, so that you can turn your ear to the sound of the catcher—we'll get to that in a minute—I'm going to make you a sidearmer."

Batters hate that kind of pitcher, because the ball comes right at them before it breaks if you throw a curve or a nasty slider. When you throw over the top, the batter can pick up the spin of the ball, but sidearm, they never know what's coming.

"So, let me show you the motion. Put your hands right here." My father placed my hands on his hips and his right shoulder and framed every step of a good sidearm motion.

"All right," he said, taking his place behind home plate. "I'm going to bang my fist into the glove, and I want you to hone in on the sound. Then, when you come from the side, let your right hand go right to the target, and put some body into it. Okay, picture yourself like big Frank Sullivan. We're in Fenway Park, Boyo, and it's the seventh game of the World Series. We're playing—let's see—the Brooklyn Dodgers, and Duke Snyder is up. You know what a good eye Snyder has, so you don't want to groove the pitch. You want to nibble at the corners. All right. Let me give you the target. Remember, right hand all the way to the mitt. Let the sound guide your throw."

I was so excited as I heard my father pounding his fist into the glove. "All right, Tommy boy, throw it right in here! Here we go, kid! Hum it in right here! Let's see a little bit of that old pepper!"

Da had shown me a simple windup, and when I let the ball

go, I put all of my hundred pounds into the effort. I heard my father come out of his squat, leaping for the errant ball as it soared over his head. "Oh Jesus," he said.

And then there was a crash, followed by Peggy's cry. "Hey, Mom, Tommy broke a window! Tommy broke a window!"

In a minute, my mother was downstairs, assessing the damage.

"It's just a window," my father yelled. "We've got about— oh, let's see—fifty more of them. We probably need new ones anyway, don't we, Marie?"

My mother didn't respond, so Da went right on. "Now, Tommy," he said, "that was an excellent pitch. You're just a little excited. All pitchers are wild when they first come on the mound. We should've given ya some gentle warm-ups. So just feel the motion now, and lob the ball until you get used to it."

Over the next two hours, I threw pitches until my right arm felt like it was falling off, and by the end, I got a little better. Every time I threw that baseball, I was Frank Sullivan in Fenway Park, pitching against the Brooklyn Dodgers in the seventh game of the World Series. Each time I threw a pitch, it felt a little more natural. Every time that pitch found its mark, the more enthusiastic I got. But what did it all mean? What did my father have in mind?

I didn't learn for a few days. Somehow, after more late-night arguments, Billy was allowed to play with me again. *Maybe God does perform miracles*, I thought. All I knew for sure was that I was a happy little boy, and Billy was an excellent catcher. In two weeks, I was actually throwing strikes, and Billy's brother,

Michael, helped us out by standing up there with a bat. He
didn't hit balls—we couldn't afford more windows—but I know
that both he and Billy were impressed with my pitching. In my
topsy-turvy life, I was at the top of my game and the top of the
world, once more enthusiastically looking forward to each and
every summer day.

14 : THE GAME

THE SUNDAY MORNING CONCLAVE WAS WELL underway with my father holding court. Every one of the men had been to Mass and dutifully received the Body and Blood of Christ, with some of them taking a rather liberal sip of the wine from the chalice.

My mother served breakfast to all of these Irish toughs, and her omelets were legendary. Some of the men, requiring a little "hair of the dog that bit them," were having Bloody Marys or gin fizzes or some other morning alcohol that they justified to balance the damage of the evening before. The talk, as always, was of politics—both national and, more to the point, local—and the Red Sox, who once again were

mired in fourth place, even though The Splendid Splinter, Ted
Williams, was hitting .337.

"It's management," Joe Magrio complained. "If Tom Yawkey
wasn't so tight with a buck, he'd trade for some big-time players,
at least a solid right-hander to go along with Mel Parnell. That
man's a genius southpaw. Oh, Tommy, I wish you could see his
curveball. It breaks six feet and leaves the hitters in a daze."

Hubbub. That was the only way to describe the scene on my
father's back porch every Sunday morning during the summer.
It is said that the Irish are a people who know more than they
have the right to. They certainly are a tribe that talks and talks
and talks. And I listened to all of it, drinking it in, absorbing it,
and making it a part of my own personal history.

I was surprised to hear my father clinking his glass and asking for silence. "Gentlemen, gentlemen," he said, "I have an
announcement to make. So please give me your undivided
attention." The hubbub quieted and every eye turned curiously
toward my father.

Da had amazing charisma—an ability, even among these
Boston Irish powerbrokers, to gain their attention and hold it.
"Gentlemen," he said again, "with the Red Sox in their customary dire straits, all of us have been turning our attention
from the grand game in Fenway Park to something more
local—our Little Leaguers. As you know, the Scituate Orioles
are eight-and-one in the South Shore League with a strong
chance to win the regional championship and move on to the
grand hope of making their way to the Little League World

Series in Williamsport, Pennsylvania. As parents, we dream of
that possibility for our boys. As for me, the dream is much
smaller. I dream that my son, Tommy, might have the chance
to play in just one game."

"But Porky," Billy's dad, John Hannon, politely pleaded,
"Tommy is . . ."

My father interrupted. "Unable to see, John? That's true, but
with the help of your son, Tommy will astound you all with his
ability to throw a baseball." To my surprise, Billy just appeared
with his catcher's stuff on.

"Come out with me to the backyard, boys," my father said,
"and watch my boy throw a few."

While he had been speaking, my father moved across the
room to me and put a big arm around my shoulders. Bending
down, he whispered, "It'll be all right, Tommy. I figured it was
better not to tell you about this—what should we call it—audi-
tion? Now come on, Boyo. Be a Sullivan, and show 'em."

The whole group of men trooped out into the backyard fol-
lowing my father, and I took my place on the pitcher's mound.

Billy squatted behind the plate, pounding his fist into the
glove. "All right, Tommy boy, hum it in here! Show me that
fastball!"

My stomach started to gurgle as the nerves began to take
over. Winding up, I let it go and heard Billy spring up, knocking
the ball down as it flew high and outside away from the plate.
My father was doing play-by-play.

"Nice hands, Billy, nice hands. Well, Tom, that was a little high and outside. It's just the nerves, boy. It's just the nerves. We understand. So settle down and just play pitch and catch with Billy."

Just play pitch and catch. That's what I needed to think.

The next ball made Billy's mitt pop, and my father yelled, "Strike one!" I threw twenty-four more pitches—all in the strike zone, with the men *ooooing* and *ahhhing* appreciatively on every one of my efforts. It felt great, and I was on top of the world.

"All right, Tommy," my father said, "that's enough for now. We don't want to throw out the old right arm. Give 'em one more and go to the showers."

My last pitch was a fastball, right down the middle. "Strike three!" Da called. "That had real heat on it, Boyo. It would've taken a boy with a quick bat to get any wood on that one."

The audience applauded appreciatively as Billy escorted me back onto the porch. The men got their drinks and took their customary seats.

My father wasn't finished yet. "So, boys," he went on, still holding the floor, "now that you've been dutifully impressed with Tommy's prodigious pitching performance, we arrive at the question I'm sure that all of you are asking: how will a boy without vision play in a normal game of baseball? Well, first we'll make him a relief pitcher so that he won't have to hit in the lineup. And then we'll allow his good friend, Billy, to stand out on the pitcher's mound with him while Billy's brother, Mike, catches.

"Now let me add, Billy will not be able to help Tom in any

way with fielding his position, unless by some chance a batter hits a line drive back at the pitcher, endangering Tommy. Other than that, my son will have to handle his position with Billy just giving him directions."

An ex-fighter that my father used to manage, Tussy Russell, spoke up from the back of the porch, his speech slightly slurred. "Listen, Porky," he said, "I know you're trying to do a good thing for the kid, but this—this just isn't right. What about the parents on the other team? And the other players? How are they all gonna feel?"

My father stayed reasonable. "I'll talk to them, Tussy. I'm sure they'll understand."

Now Captain Michael Murphy of the Boston PD spoke up. "Porky, there are Little League rules to consider, and insurance on the safety of all the boys."

"I'll take responsibility for everything, Captain Michael. Anyone that's hurt when Tommy's on the mound, well, I'll pay the bill."

Commissioner Patrick Malloy of the Scituate Little League confronted my father more directly. "Thomas," he said, "this just can't happen. There's no precedent for it. We need to take this up in committee."

My father strode across the room, looming over the commissioner where he sat. "Well, Patrick," he said, "I'm a committee of one, and meeting with myself. Let me see, let me see—what is it you owe on the ponies? I'm calling your debt in right now. I think it's $4,360. Is that right? That's the number I remember."

"But, Porky," the commissioner stammered, "I don't have the money."

"I know that, Patrick. And so you can buy more time by not holding your committee meeting and letting this most worthy sporting event go forward without a hitch."

"Porky," Councilman Jim O'Neil put in, "that's blackmail."

"It certainly is, Jim, but that's my son, and I'll do anything to give him a chance to participate in life, including a little black-mail. Now let me see, I would guess that everyone on this porch owes my little bookmaking operation a fair amount. And then there are all those little secrets I keep in my head concerning every man here. So, I don't think we're going to need anymore discussion about this matter, are we, boys?"

I sensed the nodding of heads and heard the mumbled responses as the men acquiesced to my father's will.

"Now," my father went on, "the bar's open. Let's get on with our Sunday morning libations, along with good conversations and mutual fellowship."

And so, that's how it came about. The die was cast. I would be making my debut in the Scituate Little League in a twilight game on Tuesday, August 11, 1959. That date will stay in my head forever because it was, in a way, my coming-out party. And though I didn't know it then, it would set in motion a chain of events that would dynamically change my life.

Billy was scheduled to pitch that night, and he did a great job, as I sat in the dugout with the butterflies in my stomach turning into B-52 bombers. I was sweating, my hands were shaking, and I had the feeling that my entire insides were about to explode. Was I nervous? Oh, you could say that. I was nervous enough to want to throw up. I only kept my stomach under control because I would be embarrassed if I did it in front of my teammates.

As the visiting team, we batted at the top of each inning. It was in the sixth that our team got a big lift when Billy's brother, Mike, hit one out of the park to tie the game at 2–2. Billy warmed me up out in right field, and I was completely wild. I guess the adrenalin was flowing so hard that I over-threw every pitch.

My friend walked out and put his arm around me. "Listen, Tommy," he said, "I know you can do this. So settle down and make believe we're just in the yard."

Make believe we're in the yard? Who was he kidding? We were in front of the whole town of Scituate, all of them believing I couldn't do it and that my father was crazy even to put me out there.

The portable PA system crackled as the announcer reported my entrance into the game. "Now pitching for the Scituate Orioles, number twenty-nine, Tommy Sullivan!"

As the batter took his place in the box, Billy started to laugh.

"What's funny?" I asked, not thinking anything could be.

Billy leaned in close. "You should see this kid's face, Tommy. He knows you're blind, and he's panicked. I can actually see him shaking, so just throw strikes to Mike. I don't think he'll even get the bat off his shoulder."

Mike was banging the mitt, encouraging me with plenty of voice. "Come on, Tommy boy, chuck it in here! Throw it right by him!"

I took a deep breath and went into my windup. As the ball left my hand, I knew it was perfect.

"Strike one!" the umpire called.

And Billy said, "See, I told you. He didn't even move the bat. Show him a curve."

Over the last two weeks, we had worked on learning to throw a curveball. It required getting my fingers across three seams of the baseball and snapping the wrist as I released it. Every once in a while I threw it pretty well, and on this day, it was perfect.

The batter swung and missed, and Billy yelled, "He missed it by a foot, Tommy! You've got him going!"

Mike was banging his glove again, and I was beginning to gain confidence. This time, I threw a sinker that Da had taught me, and it crossed the plate right at the knees with the umpire crying, "Strike three!"

The crowd roared, with my Da's booming voice louder than anyone's. "That's the way to go, Tommy! That's the way to get in the game! Mow 'em down, Boyo! Mow 'em down!"

I walked the next batter, probably because I got too cocky. The next kid popped up. So we had two outs with a runner on first as Chucky Jones, a kid I knew pretty well, came to the plate.

Billy said, "There's something going on, Tommy. Their manager is up and making all kinds of signs with his hands. There's something fishy happening." We found out quickly what it was.

When I threw the first pitch, Chucky squared around and bunted the ball right back toward me.

Billy yelled, "To your left, Tommy, to your left! Now down. Pick it up!"

But I was too late, and everybody was safe. The crowd booed, incensed by the obvious effort on the other team's part to take advantage of my being blind. People were screaming at the umpire to do something about it. But the fact was, Chucky hadn't broken any rules. We had agreed that I had to play the game for real. And so he had bunted his way on. I was so upset that I walked the next batter. The bases were loaded when the fates stepped in and big Eddy Mullins strode up to home plate.

As Mike started to bang his fist in the mitt, Eddy began to pound his bat on the plate. "Come on, Blindey," he sneered, "throw it right in here, and I'll hit it all the way to Boston. You can't throw it by me, Blindey. Bring the heat! Let's see what you got!"

"Take it easy, Tommy," Billy said. "He's just a big windbag. I've struck him out before. He's always trying to hit it out of the park. So if you can keep the ball down and inside, his big swing can't get around on it. Just work for the inside part of the plate. You can do it, Tommy, I know you can."

Eddy was still talking. "Come on, Blindey, throw it in here!"

I threw the first pitch with all my might and heard a crack as Eddy connected. The ball flew high and long out of the park, but thank God it was foul down the left-field line. The crowd oohed and ahhed.

"Ahhh! That felt good, Blindey," Eddy said. "Throw me another one like that."

I could feel the rage building. *Why does this kid pick on me all the time? What does he have against me? Maybe nothing,* I thought. *Maybe it's just because he likes to pick on anyone different.* What I knew at that moment—what I absolutely knew—was that I hated him. On the next pitch, I threw him a curve and heard his bat whiff at nothing but air.

"Strike two!" the umpire called.

"What's the matter?" Eddy yelled. "Are you afraid to throw one right down the middle? Are you afraid I might just hit it out of the park? Come on, Blindey, give me one to swing at."

As I stood on the mound trying to control my emotions, I realized that Eddy Mullins was the thing that was standing between me and a place in the world. And I knew that if I was ever going to gain real acceptance from the other kids, I had to show them I wasn't afraid of Eddy and that I wasn't going to let him get in my way.

The count was no balls and two strikes. I could afford to waste one.

And so, as Mike pounded his glove and Eddy banged his bat on the plate, I wound up and threw a high hard one inside, right at him. I heard him hit the dirt as the ball flew past Mike, clanging off the backstop.

It didn't matter that a run scored, and we lost the game. I was more concerned with the pounding feet of the bull as he jumped up and charged the pitcher's mound. Billy leaped in front of me, grabbing him, but he couldn't stop the momentum of the big boy. We all tumbled to the ground, legs and arms thrashing. Eddy had me by the neck, and Billy had hold of Eddy.

I don't know what would have happened, but in a second, Eddy's hands jerked from their grip as my father broke up the fight with no effort at all. He had Eddy in one hand and me in the other, holding us like we were toys with our feet slightly suspended above the ground. At the same time, he was speaking to the crowd.

"Ladies and Gentlemen," he said, "it seems that these two boys—my son, Tommy, and this Eddy Mullins—need to settle a dispute that's been brewing all summer. And so, I'm announcing that two weeks from Sunday there'll be a boxing match—Marcus of Queensbury rules, of course—held in the backyard of the Sullivan house at 77 Barker Road. Food and drinks will be served, and wagers will be accepted. Come one, come all."

With that, he put our feet back on the ground and herded me away.

A boxing match? What was he talking about? I couldn't fight Eddy Mullins. I'd get killed. But my father had said it, and so I knew it would have to happen. I just hoped he had a plan.

15 ∶ THE SWEET SCIENCE

IT WAS EARLY THE NEXT MORNING, AND I HADN'T slept. All night I'd been dreaming of fighting Eddy, who had morphed into a monster with punches that pulverized my body, shattering my bones and splattering my brains.

When I awoke, I was surprised to hear the sound of hammering out in the yard even before the usual wake-up song of my friend, the robin. My Da was out there doing something, and I scrambled into my clothes to get outside and find out what was going on.

"Good morning, Boyo," he said buoyantly, "and what a fine day it is for you to learn the art of the sweet science."

"The sweet science?" I asked, not comprehending.

"That's right, Tommy boy—pugilism, fisticuffs, prizefight-ing, or, as we Irish like to say, a true donnybrook. That's why I'm out here so early on this fine morning. Actually, I haven't slept yet. It was a long night at the bar, but there's plenty of time for rest. Now, let me show you what I'm doing."

My father took my hand and ran it along strands of rope he had strung together.

"My boy," he said proudly, "I'm building a squared circle—the ring in which you're going to demolish that loudmouthed bully, Eddy whatshisname."

"Mullins," I added, not convinced. "Eddy Mullins."

"That's right," he said. "Eddy Mullins—that big blowhard of a kid who will go down with one punch. They're all like that, the bullies. If you just stand up to 'em, they melt away like a snowman in a spring thaw."

My Da sounded so confident, but that's not how I was feeling.

"How am I gonna fight him, Da?" I asked. "He's so big, and I'm . . ."

"Don't say it, Tommy. I've got it all worked out. Your eyes may not work very well, but we're going to turn you into a mongoose. Have you ever heard the story of the mongoose, Boyo? They live in *Indja*—that faraway land of Sikhs and mys-tics, where the most dangerous creature is the king cobra, whose poison kills with just one bite, except when he comes up against the mongoose. You see, the mongoose knows just how to lash out and catch the head of the viper in its jaws, crushing it before it has a chance to strike. That's how we're going to train you, Boyo—to be a mongoose.

"And there's a famous pugilist I want to tell you about, who used this philosophy to become a great champion, holding his titles well into his forties—the same age I am today. His name was Archie Moore, Tommy, and there was never a boxer like him. You'll learn a lot more about him in a little while, but first I have something else to show you."

Da went to the corner of the yard and came back carrying something in his arms.

"Take a look at these, Boyo," he said, placing two objects in my hands.

What felt like pillows turned out to be something much more important.

"Those are boxing gloves, my boy, but not just ordinary gloves. Those were worn by the mongoose, Archie Moore himself, the night he won the light heavyweight championship of the world—for the third or maybe the fourth time, I might add. Archie gave them to his trainer, but because the man fell on rather hard times and happened to owe me a considerable amount of money in back bets, I acquired these gloves, and now you'll wear them. There's magic in them, Tommy boy, with lightening in your left hand and thunder in your right. And so, we are here this morning with your first lesson in the sweet science."

While Da laced on the gloves, he continued to regale me with stories about the pugilistic conquests of the mongoose, Archie Moore, and began to describe the technique I would use to take out big Eddy Mullins.

"It begins with understanding the basic concept. The mongoose never wastes energy, protects himself, and strikes only when the time is right. So what we want to learn first is to find the secret power in a punch well delivered—a fatal blow that brings an opponent to his knees. We'll start with the left hand and master the use of the jab.

"Now first, about your posture. I want you in a crouch with your chin tucked deep into your chest like this."

My father placed me in the position.

"Get your hands up high with your elbows out at a ninety degree angle. That's it. Now keep that head tucked down and your weight on the balls of your feet so you can move and bounce laterally. Now let's work on the bounce. Ready? Here we go.

"Bounce. Bounce. That's it. Good. Light on your feet. Bounce with me. Bounce with me."

My father moved me around the yard in bouncing circles, always moving clockwise. "You always want to be moving clockwise, Tommy boy, to stay away from big Eddy's right hand, and we need you to be stepping slightly forward, in order to close the gap between you and him, making it so his punches have to be short. You never want him to get you out on the end of a haymaker. That's the one danger. That's how he might knock you out. But if you keep your head tucked in and stay in your crouch, he doesn't have much of a target to punch at, does he?

"About the jab. In your case, I want you to think of it like a snake's tongue. You're going to flick it out, flick it out, so that you can find and measure your opponent like this."

My father got behind me and moved my left arm in a flicking motion, like he said, making believe that it was the tongue of a viper.

"Keep bouncing, Boyo. Keep bouncing. Now, when you've got him measured, you're going to come out of your crouch, driving with your legs and putting your weight behind your punches. Like this."

My father pushed me so hard that I fell forward onto the grass, landing with a rather unceremonious thud.

"I'm sorry, Boyo," he said. "Are you all right?"

"Sure, Da, sure," I answered, clamoring back to my feet and shaking off the grass.

"Okay," he said, "now I'll be Eddy. Let's begin to spar and work out the kinks."

Over the next ten minutes, I tried to be a snake with my jab, a mongoose with my defense, and a power puncher when I struck at my Da. Most of the time I waved at midair. Every once in a while, I felt the connection when my punches landed on my father's chest or arms.

After a while, he said, "Look, Tommy, this isn't quite the way it should be because I'm too tall. Let me get down on my knees where you can punch at me on the same level. Now I'm also going to hit you a little so that you can learn to keep your guard in place."

And he did. Actually, he hit me pretty hard, wanting me to feel the impact of a glove in my face.

"You gotta learn to take it as well as give it, boy," he said.

"This Eddy Mullins is gonna try and knock your block off, and when you're in there, you have to hit him."

I knew that wasn't going to be any problem. Eddy had picked on me from the first time I had met him, and I wanted—no, I needed to win—for reasons that went well beyond the fight itself.

My Da was baiting me, trying to get me angry. "Come on, Tommy," he chided. "Is that all you've got? Can't you hit me any harder than that? What's the matter? Are you a sissy? Come on. Show me something! See, I'll even put my hands down at my sides and give you an open target to hit. Aw, that's nothing. That felt like a girl's slap."

Da was really getting under my skin. The next time I flashed out of my crouch as the mongoose, there was real purpose in my effort.

BANG!

I really nailed my Da. Right on the chin. He grunted, and the force of the blow rolled him right back onto the grass. I was immediately sorry.

"Are you all right, Da? Are you all right?"

My father was laughing. "That was a great shot, Boyo," he said, hugging me. "You knocked me right on the old keister. If you nail this big palooka with a shot like that, why, the referee will count to ten, and he'll still be on his back looking up at the stars. How did it feel, Tommy? Did ya like it?"

"I loved it," I told him. "It felt great."

And it did. For a little while, the cloud of fear was swept away, and I basked in the delight of my pugilistic accomplishments.

As we shared a lemonade sitting on the back porch, Da went on to tell me that this was just a first step in my training. Over the next two and a half weeks, I would be weight lifting, jogging, eating big breakfasts, and getting a lot of sleep.

"A boxer has to be as mentally prepared as he does physically, Tommy," my father told me. "I want you to picture yourself knocking Eddy Mullins out. No more bad dreams, right, Boyo? Only dreams of conquest, accomplishment, and glory."

We trained every morning, starting at five o'clock with roadwork and a swim. Then there was breakfast, followed by lifting weights and sparring. My father never missed the opportunity to encourage me, while my mother said nothing. She was silent, never speaking about the fight, and our house seemed cold with a chill between my parents that threatened to shatter their marriage and our lives.

It was Friday night, two days before the big fight. I'd been with Billy all day. He'd helped me with my roadwork in the morning and sparred with me in the afternoon, with my Da prompting him to not hold back and pull his punches.

"Get in there and hit him, Billy. For God's sake! He's not going to be playing patty-cake when big Eddy's in the ring. Pop him!"

And reluctantly my friend did, giving me a bloody nose in the process. I landed a few good licks myself and really thought that the Archie Moore peek-a-boo style was working pretty well.

Billy stayed for dinner, but I was surprised when my mother told him he had to go home and wouldn't be allowed to sleep over that night. She just said, "Tommy needs his rest, Billy," and that was the end of it. I watched TV until about nine o'clock and was again a little surprised when I went upstairs to get ready for bed and found my mother in my room.

"Stay dressed, Tommy," she said, sharply. "You're not going to be sleeping here tonight."

"What do you mean?" I asked, not understanding.

"You and I are leaving and going to Boston to live with your grandmother."

What is she talking about? Live with Grandmother?

"But, Mum, I don't want to go anywhere. I love it right here in Scituate with Billy. And besides, don't you remember? There's the big fight Sunday with Eddy. I can't go anywhere now. I have to fight Eddy."

"You don't have to do any such thing, Tommy. It's madness for a boy who's blind to box. Your father's—well, he's wrong about this. I'm not going to let you get hurt. There will be no fight. Now help me carry these suitcases down to the car."

"No!" I yelled. "I'm not going anywhere. I'm staying right here with Da, and I'm going to fight Eddy Mullins on Sunday."

My mother tried to be reasonable. "Listen, Tommy, I think it's a brave thing, what you're trying to do. I know it's because you want to be like the other boys. I understand that. You want them to like you and make you a part of the neighborhood. But the truth is, there are things a blind boy shouldn't do—or rather, can't do—and boxing, well, that's certainly one of those things."

"You're wrong, Mum!" I exploded. "You're wrong. I can do

anything. Da says I can do anything I want to if I just work hard and believe."

"That's not quite true," my mother said, softly. "There are some things, Tommy, that you have to be able to see to accomplish. But you can have—you will have a rich and full life. You are very talented and special, and I know you'll succeed, but it has to be done in the right way, not doing something as stupid as getting into a ring and fighting with a boy who's twice your size."

I felt, rather than heard, my father's presence loom in the bedroom doorway. His voice was soft, velvet, almost warm, but I sensed a coldness of icy resolve.

"You know what they say, Marie, the bigger they are, the harder they fall. That's what I've been telling Tommy, and that's what he believes."

I stood at the edge of the bed with my mother and father opposite me on the other side. I sensed that they were close together, facing each other, and I could hear both of them breathing hard with the tension building in the air. They reminded me of two boxers facing off in a fight over what—over me.

"So, what are the suitcases for, Marie?" my father asked. "Are you taking a trip?"

"You might as well know it, Porky. I'm leaving you and taking Tommy to my mother's."

"Oh? Well, when would you be going?"

"Tonight."

Tonight. I heard my mother take two steps and then stop abruptly as my father moved directly in front of her.

"I don't think that will be possible, Marie," he said, his tone becoming even more soft and reasonable. "You see, Tommy and I have some work to do on Sunday afternoon. You must have forgotten about that."

Now my mother turned to me, trapped by my father and the bed.

"Go downstairs, Tommy, and get in the car. I'll be right there."

I could feel the tears starting to well up in my eyes and knew I was about to cry.

"No, Mum," I said. "I'm not going with you. I'm staying here with Da and Peggy and fighting Eddy Mullins."

"Get in the car!" she yelled. "Go downstairs and get in the car."

"No!" I screamed. "No!"

"You heard the boy, didn't you, Marie? He couldn't have said it plainer. He's staying here."

"With you, Porky, and all of your drunken friends? That's a great environment for him, isn't it? How do you think he'll grow up then, Porky? Maybe with a tin cup and a cane on the streets of Boston, or making music in some cheap bar? And who are you going to get to take care of him when you're not home for days at a time? Who is going to love him? Some bar bimbo?"

"I am, Marie, the way I always have."

"You never loved him, Porky. Not really. You weren't even here when he was born."

"Oh, we're going to talk about that again, are we, Marie? The trip I was on to Florida. You're going to blame me for Tommy's infirmity?"

"That's right, Porky. You still can't say it, can you? You think it's something about your manhood. You call him sightless, handicapped, infirmed, disabled. That's not what he is, Porky. Your son is . . ."

"Shut up, Marie. My son is what I'll make him."

"Oh yes, you will, Porky. You'll make him in your image and likeness because you can't accept who he really is. You never could." I heard my mother take a deep breath. "Your son is blind!"

The word crackled in the air like a gunshot. My father grabbed my mother and pushed her against the wall.

"Don't you ever say that, Marie. Don't you ever use that word again, or I'll kill you."

"He's blind!" my mother screamed. "Blind! Blind! Blind!"

I came around the bed and ran headlong, smashing into my father's chest and knocking him off balance.

"Stop it! Stop it!" I screamed. "Listen to me. For once, will you please listen to me?"

We all were silent for a minute, trying to gather ourselves. I went on, crying, working to get the words out.

"I'm blind, but I'm Tommy, and there's a lot of things that Tommy wants to do and be, and you—not either one of you—will listen to me. Maybe I want to be a lawyer or a teacher or a cowboy or a baseball player. I don't know. But what I already know is that I want to be me, and I want to be like other little boys. I want to play with them and go to school with them. I want to be a 'normie' like them, and neither of you really ever listens to me. You just pull me back and forth and back and forth.

It's not just about what you think—what you say. Somebody has to pay attention to what I want. Mum, I'm staying here. Da, I'm going to fight Eddy."

I heard my mother crying as she raced out of my room, slamming the door of her own bedroom and locking it. Da tried to hug me, but I pushed him away and crumpled onto my bed, overwhelmed with emotion. He stood there for a moment, looking down at me, and then turned. I heard his feet heading heavily down the stairs, and then there was blessed silence.

16 : THE FIGHT

THE NIGHT BEFORE THE FIGHT SEEMED ENDLESS. I tossed and turned and dozed, and when I dreamed, Eddy, the giant, was killing me. Reluctantly, my mother had let Billy stay over, and I thought he was sleeping soundly in the other twin bed until he asked me a question in the dark.

"Tommy, you awake?"

"Yeah."

"Can I have all of your forty-fives?"

"What? What are you talking about, Billy?"

"Your record collection. Can I have it after Eddy kills you?"

"That's not funny," I said.

"I know," he said, concern registering in his voice. "But I

think that's what's gonna happen. You're gonna get smooshed."

I don't know why, but I got up, and being comfortable in the dark I walked through the house and out the back door in my pajamas, crossing the yard and going to the fence that had for so long kept the world outside and kept me a prisoner within.

I grabbed the chain link and shook the fence, trying to rip it out of the ground. I suppose I would have continued pulling and tugging at the hated wire, but I felt Billy's hand on my shoulder.

"What are you doing out here, Tommy?"

I turned to my friend, still clutching the fence.

"You know why I hate this fence, Billy?" I asked, feeling angry tears forming behind my eyes. "Because I know that out there is the real world that I want to become a part of. There's so much stuff I don't know about, so much I have to learn. Do you remember when we were out fishing, and I asked you to tell me about colors and rainbows?"

"Yeah. I remember."

"Well, that's just some of the things I don't know about. I'm blind, Billy, not stupid. I just see things in a different way than you do. There's so many things I want to understand."

We were both quiet for a minute, listening to the night sounds. Billy finally broke the silence.

"So why do you have to fight Eddy?" he asked.

"I don't really know, Billy," I said. "I guess because there will always be an Eddy—some big jerk who thinks that I'm not as good as he is."

I was overcome by emotion and blurted out, "Billy, I want to be just like everybody else. I want people to think that I'm just like everyone else."

Again, we were quiet, except for the soft sound as I allowed myself to cry.

Billy awkwardly put his arm around me and patted my shoulder.

"Okay, Tommy," he said. "Let's try to get some sleep. Tomorrow you'll fight Eddy, and you'll beat him. I know you'll beat him." As we walked back to the house in the dark, I wish I had felt as confident as my friend.

The day dawned, pristine and clear, and the people began to gather early for the noontime assassination of Tommy Sullivan. And boy, did they show up—by the hundreds. I suppose it was the thirst for blood or something, but I couldn't believe that this many residents of Scituate would gather in my backyard to see two little boys fight. It was long afterward that I found out why. My father, never missing a business opportunity, was taking bets on the fight. Years later, Billy told me that the pot was pretty big.

"It's amazing, Tommy," he said, as I waited in the house. "Your dad's out there on the porch, and the line's around the block."

Just then, my Da came in. "Well, are you ready, champ, to send this big palooka to Queer Street? When you flash out like the mongoose and nail him with that good right hand, why, the referee'll count to ten, and he'll still be lying there. Now let's get the gloves laced up. Oh, and I have something for you, something very special."

My father produced a box that he opened.

"Wow," Billy said. "It's a robe, Tommy. It's awesome."

"A fighter's robe, Boyo," my father said. "And on the back it has your name with a moniker to describe the way you'll fight. It reads, "Tommy 'The Cyclops' Sullivan." Do you know who the Cyclops was, Boyo? He was a giant in Greek mythology with one eye in the middle of his head—a warrior of great renown, who slew his enemies with one swipe of his sword. Actually, he was kind of a bad giant, but for our purposes, we'll overlook that fact. Let's see how it fits."

My father slipped the robe over my shoulders, and I tried not to shake with nerves.

"Da, can I wait a minute to put the gloves on? I need to go to the bathroom." And boy, did I have to go.

"Ah, you've got the nerves going," my father said. "That's good. All champions get nervous before they accept a challenge. Well, don't worry about a thing. You go use the bathroom there, and Billy and I will wait for you."

I felt sick. I felt really sick. I wasn't just nervous, I was scared. I was going to fight a kid who was almost twice my size, and not for the first time that morning I remembered that I was blind.

After spending quite a while in the bathroom, I seemed to get my stomach under control, and like they promised, Da and Billy were waiting outside.

"All right, it's time, Boyo. Let's put on the gloves. Actually, it's been very good—you're going into the bathroom like that.

I've seen Eddy out there, walking up and down, shadowboxing and punching the bag a little. I think you've got him worried."

I don't think so, I thought. *I don't think so at all.*

Billy and Da would be in my corner, and Da's head bartender, the ex-fighter, Tussy Russell, would be the referee.

The crowd actually roared as I came out the back door of the house and down the steps.

My father stopped on his way to the ring. "I have another surprise for you, Tommy—two of your very special friends who wanted to be here to see you fight today."

I was amazed. It was Jerry and Ernie. I was even more surprised when Ernie said, simply, "Remember, Tommy, you're fighting for us today. We're here because you're fighting for us."

I almost wanted to cry, and for a minute I wasn't afraid. "Where's Mum?" I asked. "Is she here in the crowd?"

"I don't know, Tommy," my Da said, soberly. "You understand, your mother doesn't feel the same way about this that we do."

We had come to the edge of the ring, and I ducked under the ropes that my father had strung. Talk about leading the lamb to the slaughter. Da was leading me to a lion waiting on the other side of the ring.

The referee called us to the center for our instructions.

"Ladies and Gentlemen," he said, yelling above the din, "you've come here today for the main event—three rounds of boxing. According to the Marcus of Queensbury rules, all rounds will be three minutes with a one-minute rest. Beansy, I mean, Jimmy Norton, will be counting for the knockdowns—

if there are any—and I'll keep the time right here on my stop-watch. You boys understand that there'll be no punching below the belt or biting in the clinches. That's where I got my cauliflower ear—when Tom McNally bit me. I'd fight him today if I could."

"Well, you're not fighting, Tussy," my father yelled. "So get on with the instructions."

"Okay, okay, Porky. They'll be no rabbit punching, and when I tell you to break, break. Now, go back to your corners and come out fighting at the bell. Good luck to both of you."

As I made my way back to the corner, my father put his arm around me.

"Listen to me, Tommy," he said. "When he first sees you in your crouch as the mongoose, he's not going to know what to do or how to hit you, so go right after him. In the beginning, surprise is on your side, so don't be afraid, and remember every-thing I taught you. Good luck."

Da banged me on the back so hard he almost knocked me down. And then the bell rang to begin round one.

I came out into the middle of the ring with my hands up in the peek-a-boo style of the mongoose, made famous by the great Archie Moore. *But where is Eddy?* I couldn't hear him. The crowd was cheering, and I couldn't hear him breathing. *Where is he?*

"Over here, Blindey," he said. "Over here." When I turned to the sound of his voice, he had moved. "Right here, Blindey. Right here."

This time he tapped me on the head with his glove. It was

maddening. So, in frustration, I came out of my mongoose defense and took a tremendous blow to the jaw. As Eddy's punch landed, my knees buckled, and I nearly went down. But I still managed to throw out a desperation punch of my own that only hit air.

Eddy was laughing. "Want some more, Blindey? Here's some more."

His next punch grazed my chin.

"Get your hands up, Tommy," my father yelled. "Get your hands up!"

I did, and temporarily the mongoose defense worked. His next series of blows landed on my arms and shoulders, hurting. But I was able to connect with a few short punches of my own that seemed to surprise the giant, or maybe just got him mad, because as I flicked out my jab, trying to find him above the noise of the crowd, I was hit with a series of blows that sent me sprawling to the grass. Eddy stood over me.

"Come on. Get up, Blindey. Get up so I can hit you again."

"Go to your corner," the referee barked, "until I tell you to come out!"

Reluctantly, Eddy backed off as the count continued. ". . . four, five, six . . ."

I was up at the count of seven, just in time to get hit with a left hand to the stomach and a right cross Eddy must have thrown from Boston. It crashed into my chin and sent me down again. Really, honestly, I saw stars—blue ones and purple ones and pink ones—I saw them all.

I could hear the crowd yelling, "Stay down, Tommy. Stay down."

But above the noise, I could hear my father's voice. "Get up, Tommy. Get up. You're a Sullivan, Boyo. You can't let it end this way, lying on your back. You have to be on your feet with the referee holding up your hand as a winner. Now get up, Tommy. Get up!"

". . . seven, eight . . ."

Painfully, I got to a standing position at the count of nine. And gratefully, before Eddy could do any more damage, the bell rang, ending the first round.

My Da's arm was around me as he led me back to the corner. "You're doing great, Tommy," he said, "just great."

"I can't hear him, Da. There's too much noise. I can't hear him."

"Well then, we'll have to think of something. Can you get him mad, Tommy?" my father asked.

Somehow I found humor in that idea and laughed through gritted teeth. "I think he's already mad, Da."

"But can you get him to talk to you, Tommy? Then you'll know exactly where he is, and you can begin to do a little damage of your own. Listen, Tommy. Listen to me carefully. I know you can win this fight. But even if you don't, it's important that you're in it and that he understands that you're here fighting and that you're not afraid. Sometimes that's worth just as much. So go out there this round and give it your best."

The bell sounded for round two, and as I moved into the

center of the ring, I began to talk to Eddy. "Hey, fat boy," I said. "You're not so tough. You couldn't even knock out a blind kid."

"Shut up," he said. "I'll finish you off in this round."

I honed right in on the sound of his voice and flashed out of my mongoose defense, hitting him with four or five quick blows. It almost felt like my punches were bouncing off the giant because it certainly didn't hurt him or slow him down. And what I got for my trouble was another devastating body punch, followed by—I don't know—three or four blows to my face and head. I was down again, and this time I felt like I wanted to stay there. *Just let me take a nap on this grass,* I thought. *The people will all go home, and I'll just stay here and rest.* And you know, I would have done just that, except that I heard two other voices in the crowd—Jerry and Ernie.

"Get up, Tommy, get up," they were yelling. And somehow I knew I had to find a way back to my feet.

Now I was on my knees struggling. *Oh God*, it was hard struggling to my feet. How I arrived in an upright position, I'll never know. I learned that day that inner strength—the desire to achieve against overwhelming odds—can overcome any adversity.

So there I was, wobbling around in the center of the ring as the bell rang, ending round two. I must have really taken a beating in the second round because as my father helped me back to the corner, there was a profound change in his manner. He sat me on the stool, toweling off the sweat on my neck and face and wiping away some blood that was dripping from my nose.

"Drink some water, Tommy, drink some water," he said. "I think you've had enough."

What is my Da saying?

"I'm gonna throw in the towel and tell the referee to stop the fight, Tommy. It's just too much. You're taking too much punishment. And you've proved your point. I've never seen such courage, and I'm incredibly proud of you."

"No, Da. No!" I nearly screamed. "You can't stop it."

"I have to, Tommy. I can't let this go on anymore." For the first and only time, my father used the words. "You're blind, Tommy. You're a brave little boy who is blind. And this—this fight—is a fight you can't win."

We were both surprised to hear my mother's voice as she leaned into the ring. "He can't quit now, Porky. I hate this. I hate what you're doing to him, but Tommy can't quit. If he does, he'll never believe he can stand on his own. If you take this moment away from him, he may never have another chance to be equal in a world I know he so desperately wants to be a part of."

"Are you crazy, Marie?" my father snapped. "If he goes out there for the next round, he's going to get killed. I promise you. He's going to be hurt."

"He can't quit, Porky. I'm telling you. He just can't quit."

"I'm stopping this right now, Marie," my father said. "Right now."

I grabbed my Da with my gloved hands. "No, Da. No. You're not stopping it. This is my life. It's my fight, and I have to finish it."

My father looked at me, and I could tell he was crying.

"All right then, Tommy boy, one more round. Just remember . . ."

"I know, Da," I said, "be the mongoose."

The bell rang sounding round three—the most important round of my life.

"Well, Blindey," Eddy said, as we came to the middle of the ring. "You want some more, huh?"

WHAM!

He threw a hard right hand that, thank God, bounced off my arms.

"That didn't hurt, Eddy," I said. "You can't hurt me. Is that all you've got?"

Eddy threw a series of punches that weren't very effective because he was angry and not concentrating.

BANG—BANG—BANG—BANG!

The blows struck my arms, but somehow I stayed upright, and I knew exactly where he was. I flicked out my left hand, measuring him.

TOUCH—TOUCH—and then—STRIKE!

Later on, Billy said that it was the luckiest punch he'd ever seen. But you know what? Sometimes fate steps in and makes the impossible possible.

I came out of my mongoose defense and threw the right cross Da had worked so hard on with me over the last two weeks. It landed with a thud, right on big Eddy Mullins's nose. He groaned and sank to the grass as the blood spurted onto the ground.

I heard the referee counting ". . . three, four, five . . ."

The crowd was going wild.

". . . six, seven . . ."

I could pick out individual voices.

". . . eight . . ."

There was Ernie and Jerry and Billy and a lot of other guys from Eddy's gang. And then there was my mother and father, cheering louder than anyone.

". . . nine, ten!"

It was bedlam. The referee was holding my hand up in the air. "Ladies and Gentlemen," he yelled, "winner by a knockout in the third round—Tommy 'The Cyclops' Sullivan!"

I don't know how it had happened, whether it was skill, luck, or intervention from a higher power, but I had won. The referee was holding my gloved hand up in the air. Everyone had come into the ring, and I was swept up by the crowd, placed on their shoulders, and carried across the yard to the big back porch.

When my feet finally touched down on terra firma, the crowd parted as my parents finally got to me. I remember our embrace as the most loving, connective moment of my life. It wasn't just my father hugging me or my mother holding me, but for one brief, powerful instant, time froze. The feeling of family cocooned me and shut out everything else. Well, almost everything else. You see, my father still had some business to conduct, and our loving tableau was interrupted as his cronies crowded around.

"What a punch, Porky!" one was saying. "You had it right.

You must have known all along. That right hand came out of nowhere, just like old Archie Moore."

So, at the same moment my father was hugging me, he was reaching into his pocket and pulling out a large wad of bills. Something was wrong. If my Da was giving these guys money, somehow I had won, and he had lost.

"Da," I asked, not quite understanding what was going on, "why are you paying these men? I won the fight."

"I know, Boyo, I know," he said, a little sheepishly. "Have you heard the phrase 'money is the root of all evil'? Have I ever mentioned that to you before?"

"Yes," I answered.

"Well, it is," he said, now laughing quietly. "It sometimes makes a father doubt his son and outsmart himself."

I could hear him still counting out bills as he paid off someone else who had bet on me to win the fight. Da was a true gambler, and I loved him for it.

As another man pushed through the crowd for payment, my father hugged me again.

"Oh, Tommy," he said, "this is probably the first and only time I've ever lost a bet and been proud to pay the piper. What a day and what a fight."

People couldn't believe what had happened, and neither could I. Billy told me that Eddy just sat on the grass during the whole celebration, trying to figure out what had gone wrong.

I suppose neither one of us really understood the how or why of what had happened.

17 ⁝ CHANGE

FOR THE NEXT FEW DAYS, I FELT LIKE TED WILLIAMS. I was a celebrity, a neighborhood star, and for a little while, every kid in town wanted to know, hang out, or be seen with Tommy "The Cyclops" Sullivan.

The phenomenon was amazing. Our house was a three-ring circus of little boys coming and going. I actually began to tire of having so many new friends at the same time. But like all celebrities, the new fans began to go away when there wasn't another big event to get excited about.

Billy and I went back to doing all the things that had made the summer of 1959 the greatest experience of my life. The difference was that sometimes other kids shared our games. Now if we went fishing, three or four other guys would be with us, and pickup games of football, baseball, basketball, or street hockey had no problem finding enough people to make up two teams.

I could sense the days growing shorter and the nights taking on a new aspect—fall was about to arrive. I could hear the crickets chirp faster as the temperature dropped. I could feel my feet crunch early falling leaves walking through the neighborhood streets. The air was dryer and less humid, and the sun felt less direct on our shoulders.

We still had some scorchers. They called it "Indian summer" in New England, when the temperature jumped into the mid-nineties—"hurricane weather," my father used to say. It was about this time in late August a few years earlier when Hurricane Carol rolled over Scituate, knocking out power for three days and creating a great adventure for Peggy and me.

Labor Day was always the saddest day of the year in Scituate. In the morning, the town fathers hosted a big parade with homemade floats, the high school band, and a big-time costume contest. Billy and I entered by covering ourselves with cardboard and becoming boxes of the popular cereal, Wheaties. We thought we could capitalize on the "Breakfast of Champions" idea, but we didn't pick up even an honorable mention during the award ceremony. Also, the slits that Billy had cut out for his eyes didn't work well, and I kept banging into things all the way along on the parade route.

Anyway, by six o'clock Labor Day night, Scituate had become a ghost town. All of the summer residents headed home to their winter houses to get ready for the opening of school the next morning. I had been so happy over the previous weeks that I hadn't thought about going back to Perkins very much. I knew it was going to happen, but when you're really a happy kid, you don't think about sad stuff that's coming. You live in the moment, treasuring each experience.

So the first time the sadness really set in was when Billy couldn't stay for supper because he had to get his school stuff together for the next morning. I understood that Da would be driving me to Perkins, and that I would be living there Monday through Friday every week. That meant I could only play with Billy on weekends and vacations. The rest of the time, I would be back inside that fenced-in place I hated.

At the thought of this, sadness, frustration, and anger overwhelmed me. I tossed and turned all night, sometimes pounding my pillow with frustration and then breaking down, crying over what I believed would be my prison sentence.

The next morning, my mother had to wake me up three times before I would get out of bed. I didn't want to face the day. I figured if I just kept the covers over my head, I could stay right there in my little cocoon—just not get up—and maybe this day would just go away.

In the end, I couldn't overcome my mother's insistence by staying under the covers. "Tommy," she called. "Breakfast is on the table. Get up now!"

When my mother's voice took on that tone, I knew I didn't have a choice. But I couldn't understand why my mother was being so insistent that morning. I mean, my parents always drove me to Perkins sometime during the afternoon. *Why is this year different?* All I could figure was that, because I had been expelled for escaping, my jailers wanted me to show up earlier or something.

So, after fifteen minutes, I was downstairs with my back-to-school clothes on and my hair brushed. A bowl of cereal, juice, and toast was waiting for me on the table. "Hurry up, Tommy," my mother said. "Eat your breakfast. You have to get going."

Peggy was on her way out the door for her first day as a senior in high school. She stopped and hugged me. "You look very handsome, Tommy," she said. "Have a great time at school."

What is she talking about? She knew I hated going to Perkins. Something weird was going on.

The other thing that added to my confusion was that Da was up and having breakfast with me. "What a grand day it is, Tommy. There's a chill in the air, just like it ought to be when a boy goes back to school. You're going to have a great year, a great year."

They were all so happy, and I was feeling lousy.

As I finished my breakfast and pushed back from the table, it was my mother's turn to hug me, along with showing me something. "What do you think this is?" she said, putting an object in my hands.

I had no idea. It was some kind of a box, but that's all I could understand as I examined it. "Open the lid, Tommy," she said. "I think you'll figure it out when you look inside."

My hands discovered food—an apple and banana, along with some cookies and two sandwiches, all wrapped up in plastic.

"It's your lunchbox, Tommy."

"And it has your name on it," my father put in, "written right across the top, 'Tommy's Lunchbox.' Just what every boy needs to go to school."

Right then there was a knock on the door. "You better answer it, Tommy," my mother said. "It's probably for you."

With my lunchbox still in my hand, I walked to the back door and opened it.

"Are you ready?" Billy said.

"Ready for what?" I asked.

"Ready for school," he said.

Earlier that summer, Billy Hannon had uttered the three most important words I ever heard—"Want to play?" Now he was asking me if I was ready for school.

"You're going to public school with Billy," my father told me. "Your mother and I have agreed to let you try it."

I couldn't believe it. I hugged Billy and dropped my lunchbox and then ran back into the kitchen, throwing my arms around my father and then my mother. I was going to be like everybody else and go to public school.

"What about Perkins?" I asked, still not believing what was happening.

My mother took a deep breath. "Tommy," she said, "I guess if you can go a few rounds in the ring, you can go a few rounds with life. Now get on your way. You boys will be late."

I put my hand on Billy's shoulder and walked out the door, down the steps, along the front walk, and out into the street. I wasn't walking to school, I was floating. This was going to be the first day of the rest of my life. I was going to share it—in the world—with other kids. It wouldn't be easy. There would be obstacles to overcome, but for the first time, I felt confident. I had defied the odds and beaten the giant. What could ever be more difficult than that?

As we walked along together, the leaves crackling under our feet and the smell of autumn in the air, I was the happiest little boy in the world. I had a family that loved me, my hand rested on the shoulder of a best friend, and I was going to go to regular school with the rest of the "normies."

18 ⠿ REFLECTIONS

THE TELEPHONE RANG, JARRING ME OUT OF MY reverie, and I found the sound annoying—no, maddening. *Leave me alone,* I thought, as it rang again. *Just leave me alone.* Anyway, what was someone doing calling me in the middle of the night?

When it rang the fourth time, I picked up the receiver. "Hello," I said, not hiding my irritation.

"Tommy, you all right?"

"Oh sure. Sorry, Billy. What time is it?"

"About six."

"What are you talking about? I got here at nine."

"Six in the morning, Tommy. The sun's up, and it's going to be a beautiful day."

"Six in the morning? Oh my God." I shook my head and stretched, trying to get my bearings. "I guess I must have fallen asleep in the chair."

My voice had awakened Edison, and the big dog nuzzled my arm as if to say, "Good morning, master." The smallest things can be so important. I could hear my friend's concern on the phone, and I felt the love of the big animal, given directly with no hesitation.

Billy was speaking again. "Listen, Tommy, I wish you had told me when you were getting in. I woulda been there to pick you up, and I woulda stayed with you last night."

"Bill, I just wanted to be alone, and I figured coming to the old man's house was the kind of therapy I needed."

"So, how did it go?" he asked.

"I'll tell you one thing, pal. I've sure been down memory lane. Some of the memories are good, and some of them not so good. But on balance, Frank Capra had it right: it's a wonderful life. And if I haven't told you before, you've had a lot to do with making it great."

"Aw, shucks," he said. "It wasn't nuthin'." We both laughed. "When are Patty and the kids getting in?"

"Some time this afternoon. I've got a driver to pick them up."

"No way," Billy complained, his feelings hurt. "I'll be right there at the airport to get them. You cancel that car. I'll bring them to you."

"I'll tell you something, pal," I told him. "It's going to be great to feel some joy in this old house. It'll help to put everything in perspective."

"Well, guess what I've got in the trunk?" he asked.

"I don't know. A case of Jameson's?"

"Nah," he said, laughing. "A brand new whiffle ball and bat. I figured we could teach young Tom how we used to play the game. You think you can still throw a curveball?"

"You mean the old Satchel Paige ephus pitch?" I laughed. "No problem. Sully will be swinging like a rusty gate. My son's never had to try and hit my efus pitch. Hey, Bill?"

"Yeah, Tommy?"

"I'm glad you're coming down. Will Kim be with you?"

"Sure. And we're planning to stay until after the funeral."

"That's great," I said, relief sounding in my voice. I really wanted my friend and my family to be with me.

"So listen, I'll talk to you when you get here, okay?"

"I'll get them there as quick as I can," he said. Then with a serious tone, "Maybe we can go clamming and have a barbeque. I think sometimes fun is the best antidote to pain."

"I agree with you, Billy. I think you've got just the formula. See you later."

We hung up, and I stood and stretched.

"Okay, Edison, I'll let you out for a little morning constitution while I make some coffee. Then maybe we can take a walk on the beach. It's a little too cold for swimming, but I could use a little exercise."

The dog thumped his tail, as if he really knew what I was talking about. And you know what? He probably did.

Fifteen minutes later, we were walking along the sand. The tide was out, so the surface provided easy footing, allowing both of us to be relaxed and unstressed. My mind went back to Billy, and I was reminded of the phrase I'd heard long ago— "Friends for a reason, friends for a season, friends for all time." That was Billy Hannon—a true friend for all time.

Here we were in our fifties, living on different coasts, involved in very different lives, and yet the bond was as strong today as it had been oh so long ago. I was unbelievably blessed, not only to have Billy in my life, but to have fallen in love, married, and shared over thirty-five years with Patty—my wife, my partner, my friend, my soul mate, my heart. It was in my relationship with this remarkable woman that I had learned about life priorities: family, faith, and friendship.

In a few hours, they would be arriving to ease my grief and share in my father's memorial and burial, along with what I knew would be a substantial and rather raucous Irish wake. There were still enough of my father's friends around who needed to pay tribute to him in the honored Irish tradition of drink and good fellowship.

I was incredibly proud of my children. My son, Tom, had chosen to follow in my footsteps, trying to make it in the music business. He was developing into a magnificent songwriter, and I believed he really had a chance to make it all the way to the big time.

Our daughter, Blythe, fits her name, Blythe Spirit. She is joyous about life, about all that it holds and the relationships that so matter to her. My children are both people who possess great character.

Last Christmas, while we were skiing in Colorado, Blythe summed up who we are as a family. She said that family could be defined with an acronym. For All Moments In Life, Yours. Your family is the only group that's with you through it all. We cherish this bond and try to live it.

And what about faith? I had struggled to find it. Probably because early on I was angry with God for making me carry what I considered to be the cross of blindness. I had so wanted to break out of my yard and live in the world of what I used to call the "normies."

There seemed to be so many obstacles in my path, so many mountains to climb, so much prejudice to overcome, and yet, when I considered the way things had worked out, I had to believe I was one of the luckiest people in the world. Certainly I had achieved much more than anyone, including myself, had expected: I had been educated at Providence College and Harvard, and was involved in all kinds of sports, particularly wrestling. I had made a number of albums and performed all over the world. And I had landed roles on television in everything from *Mork & Mindy* and *Touched by an Angel*, to *Highway to Heaven* and *Fame*. I couldn't possibly have asked for more out of life. God had blessed me a hundredfold.

As I walked on the beach, so secure in the commitment of the big dog, it dawned on me that being blind was the best thing that had ever happened to me, and maybe that was what God had in mind. I had never met an ugly person—unless they wanted to be—and I carried no labels or prejudice based on ethnicity or heritage. As I took in the myriad smells along the ocean's edge, I understood that I appreciated four marvelous senses with levels of acuity that sighted people did not possess. God provides us all with grace to make the most of what we've been given, if we put our faith in Him and live according to His teaching.

The dog and I reached the jetty at the far end of the beach and turned around. I could feel my friend pulling on the harness, like a horse knowing he was headed back for the barn. So we picked up our pace and ran the two miles back to the house. I hadn't intended to run this morning, and my head still ached a little from the whiskey the night before, but the run felt terrific. So I considered another part of my essential philosophy—the balance between independence, dependence, and interdependence.

When my parents realized I was blind, the doctor had told them in a rather unceremonious manner that I ought to be institutionalized, and that became part of why they struggled over how I should develop. Society believed that I would always be a dependent person. I suppose, right from early childhood, I had committed to the idea of being a completely independent person. It wasn't until I was raising my own family and sharing my life with Patty that I came to understand that the world needed to spin as an interdependent planet, and it was through embracing this concept that I gained inner peace. If we were all interdependent, I reasoned, then we all must have a blend of strengths and weaknesses that can be shared with our fellow man.

I laughed out loud as we ran faster, realizing that God must have known this fundamental truth all the way back at the creation of the world. We had to accept our interdependence if peoples, nations, and individuals were ever going to truly coexist.

Yesterday afternoon I had written the obituary on my father for the *Boston Globe,* and I found myself thinking about what I might want people to say about me when I was gone: "Here lies Tom Sullivan, husband, father, humanitarian, author, singer, actor, athlete, who happened to be blind."

That's what I'd learned back in 1959—that I wanted to be a person who happened to be blind, rather than a blind person. Even in the twenty-first century, I knew that I had not quite achieved that goal. Society was still labeling, still categorizing, and still pigeonholing people with disability. But I was committed to the concept that I could turn every disadvantage into an advantage if I had faith, believed in myself, and worked hard.

In the last half mile, the sun broke through the morning fog and touched my shoulders, warming me in its light and raising my spirits. Essentially, at my core, I knew absolutely that I was an optimist, but I also understood that optimism was made possible only through the values of family, faith, and friendship. The little boy who had broken out of Perkins School for the Blind and then out of his backyard, craving the world beyond borders placed upon him, was now a man with limitless opportunity who was still, every day, seeking every possible adventure.

After some cereal, toast, two more cups of coffee, and a hot shower, I felt human again. The hangover was gone, and I figured I was ready to face the wake, the funeral, and the burial of my father. I would be giving his eulogy, and I knew it would not be easy. My mother and father had divorced, though I believed they always loved each other. Their marriage had ended, I realized, and that thought brought pangs of quiet, largely because of their disagreements over what to do with me.

It was ironic that there were still fences to climb for Tom Sullivan and others—still worlds to conquer. But I knew that much could be done if we could stimulate people with special needs to believe that society was being enlightened and that on the pillars of family, faith, and friendship, anything was possible.

Edison was already up and at the front door, whining with anticipation, minutes before Billy pulled his car into the driveway and my family got out. They loved coming to Scituate, all three of them. I suppose because they knew how much it meant to me, but I also knew that they had come to love this place—this sanctuary—almost as much as I did.

My son was the first one up the stairs, and his bear hug said much. Then there was my daughter, who looked at my eyes before she hugged me. "Hey, Dad," she said, laughing, "you can go blind if you keep drinking too much of that stuff."

"Yeah, I know, I know." I laughed. "It was a long night."

When Patty hugged me, everything was okay. Her embrace said so much about her love, commitment, bonding, and trust. In her arms I felt safe, and as I hugged her back, my own strength as a person, a husband, and a man seemed to flow back into my being.

Though I had lost my mother and father, I felt complete in the arms of the person I loved more than any other. We would grow old together, this woman and I. We would read to each other and hold each other, laugh quietly and love forever. I was sure in that moment that in God's plan, Patty was my treasured gift. As long as we were here together she would be my eyes on life's twisting journey.

Once again, night had come to Scituate, and the day had been everything I imagined. Mourning and memories had left me in a state of exhaustion, but I still couldn't sleep. Whether it was adrenaline, grief, or stress, I was the last person up in the house. Everyone had settled down, including Patty, who seemed to understand that I needed to be alone for a little while. She kissed me softly. "I love you," she said. "Wake me up when you come to bed."

I stepped out onto the deck, breathing in the ocean air, pulling it deep into my lungs and tasting it. Even with the immediacy of my father's death, I felt so alive and so full of life. I felt complete as a man, content with the place I held in the world. I was fulfilled professionally and happy—so happy—personally. My disability had long since become a blessing, rather than a curse. At that moment, I thought, *God is in his heaven. All is right with the world.*

Tomorrow a bagpiper would mournfully play "Amazing Grace" at my father's grave. As I listened to the waves rolling in below, I thought of the words of the familiar hymn: "Amazing grace, how sweet the sound that saved a wretch like me; I once was lost but now am found, 'twas blind, but now I see." My adventures in darkness had become my life in the light.

EPILOGUE : AUTHOR'S NOTES

I FELT THE LITTLE BOY'S PRESENCE STANDING IN front of me and sensed that he was looking up at me with wide-eyed innocence. I always try to focus on the sound of people's voices, making their visual contact with me more comfortable, but in this case the kid wasn't saying anything, and so to him I must have looked weird. He finally asked me a question in his drawling Texas accent.

"Mr. Sullivan?" he asked.

"Yes, Jason?"

"Can you see me, Mr. Sullivan?"

"No, I can't, Jason," I said, very much used to this kind of question but appreciating his directness. "I can't see you, Jason, because I'm blind."

"Oh," he said, drawing out the word, as if he understood the significance. After a pause he went on.

"Mr. Sullivan?"

"Yes, Jason?"

"So, what's the matter with your eyes?"

Now I understood. No one had explained to Jason that I was blind.

"My eyes are broken, Jason," I told him. "They don't work. That's what the word *blind* means."

"Broken," he said, working hard to understand the true meaning of the word.

"That's right," I said, feeling like we were starting to communicate. "They're broken, like—let's see—like a broken toy."

Consider the fact that a child's brain, especially a smart one like this four-year-old's, is as large as ours. The only difference in our brains is the amount of clutter we adults have stored in there. So Jason's brain was really working overtime to understand this concept of blindness.

Finally, he came to a conclusion and clapped his hands.

"Well," he pronounced with excitement in his voice, "want me to wind them up?"

My beautiful four-year-old friend, Jason, was bringing a child's curiosity to a disability that fascinates, intimidates, and confuses those of you with sight. From the time I was a very little child, I heard all the questions:

"How do blind people dream?"

"What colors do you see?"

"Do blind people hear better than everyone else?"

"Are all of your senses more acute than ours?"

"Are you all very musical?"

"Do you have phenomenal memories?"

And even "Are you all psychic?"

The truth is, to almost all of these questions the answer is no, but they suggest how little people really understand when it comes to the state of blindness, and from that place of misinformation arises disinformation and a belief that we are either superior beings from another world or invalids who live in this one. What's accurate is that most of us are ordinary people attempting to cope with an extraordinarily complex disability. Are we all optimists? Absolutely not. But are we generally angry as we carry the cross of our disability? Not at all.

This book is a testimony to a little boy who desperately wanted to become part of the world at large. In his process of growth, he experienced prejudice and friendship in equal measure. His family, like all families of special needs children, struggled to help him find a path to success. His life adventures molded his character and made him a person who has come to love his life.

When I was born in 1947, my parents went through all the emotions common to facing the reality that they had a blind child. First, they were worried. It all began when my mother shined a light into my eyes, and I didn't react. Then, there was trying to get me to follow movement in a room or react to bright colored balls and toys hung above my crib. At some point, there was the required visit to an ophthalmologist and the pronouncement that devastates any loving mother and father: "Mr. and Mrs. Sullivan, your son is blind."

This doctor was a famous ophthalmologist at Massachusetts General Hospital in Boston. His name was Frederick Verhoeff, a German whose bedside manner failed to anticipate the emotional impact of the news he would give. Without any preamble, he looked at my parents and said, "Your son is blind. Institutionalize him."

Imagine the devastation. First, all parents are in denial. *This just can't be true. There must be another option.* Then they grieve at the loss of a perfect child. Often they blame each other, as my mother and father did. And then there is the question of where to turn for help. Ophthalmologists, then and now, do not understand how much support families really need at this most critical moment of pain and loss.

So, how do you raise a blind child? In 1947, there was nothing written on the subject and nowhere to turn for counsel or direction. Today, we know much more about a blind child's development, but even in the knowing there are still so many things that are frightening.

In my examination of the state of blindness, I was amazed to learn that almost all blind children tend to crawl backward because they're afraid of hitting their heads. They also give the impression of being very placid babies when they are in their cribs, because they are desperately afraid of motion and even physical contact. Many of them are touch-adverse or overreact to the stimulation of the simplest sound. I was amazed to learn that chewing is a visual response. A blind child has to be taught even that basic requirement of survival.

My parents faced a Herculean task when trying to figure out how to support my early development. Today, people with disabilities are blessed with all kinds of life options, yet much of the past remains the same.

So, how far have we really come? Well, thanks to the efforts of former Senator Robert Dole, a disabled person himself, and others, the Americans with Disabilities Act was passed during the decade of the seventies. It provided for the elimination of discrimination in access to housing, public facilities, and the workplace.

Then why is it that in the twenty-first century, only approximately 20 percent of all adults with disabilities who could work are actually employed? Laws, in and of themselves, do not eliminate the stigma of prejudice or bigotry. It is with knowledge and understanding of blindness that society at large will dissolve its fear of the disability.

The Education Act became the companion to the Americans with Disabilities Act in the early eighties. It provides for inclusive mainstreaming without limitation for every American child, regardless of their disability. So, why is it that special needs kids, for the most part, are still restricted to special, isolated classroom situations on almost all public school campuses?

I understand that a child with a disability requires ongoing, special support, but to ask a SPED—special education teacher— to develop curriculum when her classroom is filled by children with all kinds of unique needs seems to be impossible. No matter how many aides are provided, the quality of individualized education has to suffer.

The effort by good and sincere educators to cope utilizes a concept called IEP—Individual Education Plan. The theory is great—that every child will have a curriculum developed specifically to fill their individual needs—but with the system being overcrowded and underfunded, individual education plans often fall short.

The major breakdown, however, in the matrix of disability is in the area of socialization. Particularly among blind children, there are very few who are as fortunate as I was to find a Billy Hannon, their first friend. Most are imprisoned by their disability and never discover their own special tickets out of darkness.

The efforts of parents, teachers, administrators, and other caring Americans must be geared to bringing disability into our society at the grassroots, one-on-one level.

The classroom must be integrated by placing special needs children right into the mainstream at every possible opportunity. Why, for example, can't a blind child share a music class with his or her sighted peers? We also must work to promote after-school activities (i.e., sports teams, Girl Scouts, Boy Scouts, 4-H Clubs, along with Boys and Girls Clubs) and must find ways to provide individual accommodations if the next generation of Tom Sullivans are ever going to have a chance to take their equal and rightful place in an inclusive society.

Churches and faith-based organizations can also do so much more. If God made us in his image and likeness, should we not, in faith, embrace those of us who have borne the burden of disability? It comes down to one child being mentored, touched, and supported by the community at large. Don't walk by what makes you uncomfortable. Reach out and touch those who are less fortunate because the gift of love will be returned tenfold.

We all need to do a much better job in supporting families in their ongoing battle with disabilities. The national average for divorce in this country is around 45 percent of all Americans. Last year's statistics on families with disabilities shocked me. Eighty-two percent of couples raising a special needs child suffer through the pain and anguish of separation and divorce. Those of us who have never raised one of these special children can never really understand the stress experienced between husbands and wives in these unique circumstances.

So let me be perfectly clear, the state of disability in America is not that different from it was in 1947 when I was born. We have many more tools to work with based on access, but what goes on in the hearts and minds of American citizens is a much darker, more difficult picture to understand.

I remember celebrating the passage of the Americans with Disabilities Act and thinking, like the old spiritual says, *A change is going to come.* I wasn't naive, but I believed that over time people would amalgamate with their individual prejudices forgotten. The truth is, it hasn't happened. Much like the Civil Rights Movement, the law has very little to do with the polarization of people in their hearts.

So, where is the bridge that will allow us to walk across

the chasm of bigotry and fear? It's found in our faith, in the acknowledgement that we are all the same in God's sight.

Dr. King had it right when he noted that people should be measured, not by the color of their skin, but by the content of their character.

I've been blessed to know thousands of disabled people who are completely able. Through the strength of their character, they are ready to take their rightful place in our society at all levels, both professionally and personally. I am convinced that within every person coping with a disability, God has provided an ability that will allow each of them to live active and productive lives.

You may be saying, *That can't be true, Tom. How can a person living with the complexity of disability ever achieve a level of happiness and contentment?*

It's all about the power of love because, in fact, God designed the world, not as a place of independence or dependence, but as a sanctuary of our interdependence.

We all need each other in love, support, survival, and faith. This is God's plan for all of us. I believe we are given the grace to celebrate our own uniqueness and take our rightful place as equals in an equal world.

Everyone is a contributor in God's sight, and everyone has a place here to be shared through purpose and love.

TO MY THOMAS NELSON FAMILY:

To Jonathan Merkh—for having a vision to help me bring my vision forward and make *Adventures in Darkness* the greatest creative experience of my life.

To Brian Hampton—your care and intelligence made me believe that editors truly do care about the writers they work with.

To Bryan Norman—intelligence and goodness are not wasted on the young. I'm very proud of the work we shared and delighted by our friendship.

To Dave Schroeder—you make marketing fun and also helped me fulfill the dream that means so much personally.

To Stephanie Newton—every day I appreciate the efforts you make to sound the clarion call of publicity that allows me to bring *Adventures* forward to the public.

To Jan Miller & Associates—every creative person hopes for representation that reflects the hopes and dreams of the work. In every way, you're an agent's agent and a friend's friend.

To the ladies of EDA—Julie, you make it possible for me to bring my writing out of the darkness into the light. Thank you. Thank you.

To the Thomas Nelson sales force—without you, fulfilling a dream would not be possible; I look forward to bringing more of my work to you over the years. Thank you.